PRAISE FOR

Getting to
YES

"*Getting to YES* has an unrivaled place in the literature of dispute resolution. No other book in the field comes close to its impact on the way practitioners, teachers, researchers, and the public approach negotiation."
—NATIONAL INSTITUTE FOR DISPUTE RESOLUTION FORUM

"*Getting to YES* is a highly readable and practical primer on the fundamentals of negotiation. All of us, as negotiators dealing with personal, community, and business problems, need to improve our skills in conflict resolution and agreement making. This concise volume is the best place to begin."
—JOHN T. DUNLOP

"This splendid book will help turn adversarial battling into hardheaded problem solving." —AVERELL HARRIMAN

"*Getting to YES* is a highly readable, uncomplicated guide to resolving conflicts of every imaginable dimension. It teaches you how to win without compromising friendships. I wish I had written it!" —ANN LANDERS

"*Getting to YES* is powerful, incisive, persuasive. Not a bag of tricks but an overall approach. Perhaps the most useful book you will ever read!" —ELLIOT RICHARDSON

"Simple but powerful ideas that have already made a contribution at the international level are here made available to all. Excellent advice on how to approach a negotiating problem."
—CYRUS VANCE

PENGUIN BOOKS

Getting to
YES

The authors of this book have been working together since 1977.

ROGER FISHER is Williston Professor of Law *Emeritus* at Harvard Law School, Founder and Director *Emeritus* of the Harvard Negotiation Project, and the Founding Chair of the Program on Negotiation at Harvard Law School. Raised in Illinois, he served in World War II with the U.S. Army Air Force, in Paris with the Marshall Plan, and in Washington, D.C., with the Department of Justice. He has also practiced law in Washington and served as a consultant to the Department of Defense. He was the originator and executive editor of the award-winning television series *The Advocates*. He has consulted widely with governments, corporations, and individuals. He is the author or coauthor of numerous prize-winning scholarly and popular books, including his most recent: *Beyond Reason: Using Emotions as You Negotiate.*

WILLIAM URY is cofounder of Harvard's Program on Negotiation and Distinguished Fellow of the Harvard Negotiation Project. Raised in California and Switzerland, he is a graduate of Yale and Harvard, with a doctorate in social anthropology. Ury has served as a mediator and advisor in negotiations ranging from wildcat strikes to ethnic wars around the world. He was a consultant to the White House on establishing nuclear risk reduction centers in Washington and Moscow. His most recent project is Abraham's Path, a route of cross-cultural travel in the Middle East that retraces the footsteps of Abraham, the progenitor of many cultures and faiths. Ury's most recent book is *The Power of a Positive No: Save the Deal, Save the Relationship, and Still Say No.*

BRUCE PATTON is Cofounder and Distinguished Fellow of the Harvard Negotiation Project, cofounder of the Program on Negotiation at Harvard Law School, and a founder and partner of Vantage Partners, LLC, a consulting firm that helps Global 2000 companies negotiate and manage their most critical relationships. As a mediator, he helped structure the settlement of the U.S.–Iranian hostage conflict, worked with Nobel Peace Prize winner Óscar Arias to ensure the success of the Arias Peace Plan for Central America, and worked with all parties in South Africa helping to create the constitutional process that ended apartheid. A graduate of Harvard College and Harvard Law School, he is also coauthor of the *New York Times* bestseller *Difficult Conversations: How to Discuss What Matters Most.*

BOOKS BY ROGER FISHER

Beyond Reason: Using Emotions as You Negotiate
(with Dan Shapiro, 2005)

Lateral Leadership: Getting Things Done When You're NOT the Boss
(with Alan Sharp, 1998)

*Coping with International Conflict: A Systematic Approach to Influence in
International Negotiation* (with Andrea Kupfer Schneider,
Elizabeth Borgwardt, and Brian Ganson, 1996)

Beyond Machiavelli
(with Elizabeth Kopelman and Andrea Kupfer Schneider, 1994)

Getting Together: Building Relationships As We Negotiate
(with Scott Brown, 1988)

Improving Compliance with International Law (1981)

International Mediation: A Working Guide; Ideas for the Practitioner
(with William Ury, 1978)

International Crises and the Role of Law: Points of Choice (1978)

Dear Israelis, Dear Arabs: A Working Approach to Peace (1972)

International Conflict for Beginners (1969)

International Conflict and Behavioral Science: The Craigville Papers
(editor and coauthor, 1964)

BOOKS BY WILLIAM URY

*The Power of a Positive No:
Save the Deal, Save the Relationship, and Still Say No* (2007)

Must We Fight? (editor and coauthor, 2001)

The Third Side: Why We Fight and How We Can Stop (2000)

Getting Past No: Negotiating in Difficult Situations (1991, revised edition 1993)

*Windows of Opportunity: From Cold War to Peaceful
Competition in U.S.–Soviet Relations*
(edited with Graham T. Allison and Bruce J. Allyn, 1989)

Getting Disputes Resolved: Designing Systems to Cut the Costs of Conflict
(with Jeanne M. Brett and Stephen B. Goldberg, 1988)

Beyond the Hotline: How Crisis Control Can Prevent Nuclear War (1985)

BOOKS BY BRUCE PATTON

Difficult Conversations: How to Discuss What Matters Most
(with Douglas Stone and Sheila Heen, 1999, 2nd Edition 2010)

Getting to
YES

NEGOTIATING AGREEMENT
WITHOUT GIVING IN

by ROGER FISHER
and WILLIAM URY
with BRUCE PATTON, EDITOR

• REVISED EDITIONS BY •
FISHER, URY, AND PATTON

PENGUIN BOOKS

PENGUIN BOOKS
Published by the Penguin Group
Penguin Group (USA) Inc., 375 Hudson Street, New York, New York 10014, U.S.A.
Penguin Group (Canada), 90 Eglinton Avenue East, Suite 700, Toronto,
Ontario, Canada M4P 2Y3 (a division of Pearson Penguin Canada Inc.)
Penguin Books Ltd, 80 Strand, London WC2R 0RL, England
Penguin Ireland, 25 St Stephen's Green, Dublin 2, Ireland (a division of Penguin Books Ltd)
Penguin Group (Australia), 250 Camberwell Road, Camberwell,
Victoria 3124, Australia (a division of Pearson Australia Group Pty Ltd)
Penguin Books India Pvt Ltd, 11 Community Centre, Panchsheel Park, New Delhi – 110 017, India
Penguin Group (NZ), 67 Apollo Drive, Rosedale, Auckland 0632,
New Zealand (a division of Pearson New Zealand Ltd)
Penguin Books (South Africa) (Pty) Ltd, 24 Sturdee Avenue,
Rosebank, Johannesburg 2196, South Africa

Penguin Books Ltd, Registered Offices:
80 Strand, London WC2R 0RL, England

First published in the United States of America by Houghton Mifflin Company 1981
Published in Penguin Books 1983
Second edition published 1991
This third edition published 2011

32nd Printing

Copyright © Roger Fisher and William Ury, 1981, 1991
Copyright © Roger Fisher, William Ury, and Bruce Patton, 2011
All rights reserved

Research at Harvard University is undertaken with the expectation of publication. In such publication the authors alone are responsible for statements of fact, opinions, recommendations, and conclusions expressed. Publication in no way implies approval or endorsement by Harvard University, any of its faculties, or by the President and Fellows of Harvard College.

LIBRARY OF CONGRESS CATALOGING-IN-PUBLICATION DATA
Fisher, Roger, 1922–
Getting to yes : negotiating agreement without giving in / by Roger Fisher, William Ury,
and Bruce Patton. — 3rd ed.
p. cm.
ISBN 978-0-14-311875-6 (pbk.)
1. Negotiation. I. Ury, William. II. Patton, Bruce. III. Title.
BF637.N4F57 2011
158'.5—dc22 2011006319

Printed in the United States of America
Set in Sabon with Eras

To our fathers,

WALTER T. FISHER, MELVIN C. URY,
and WILLIAM E. PATTON,

who by example taught us
the power of principle.

Preface to the
Third Edition

Thirty years have now passed since the initial publication of *Getting to YES*. We are delighted and humbled that so many people from so many places around the world continue to find it helpful in transforming their conflicts and negotiating mutually satisfying agreements. Little did we know at the time of its publication that this slender book would become a reference point in a quiet revolution that has over the course of three decades changed the way we make decisions within our families, organizations, and societies.

The negotiation revolution

A generation ago, the prevailing view of decision-making in most places was hierarchical. The people at the top of the pyramids of power—at work, in the family, in politics—were supposed to make the decisions and the people at the bottom of the pyramids to follow the orders. Of course, the reality was always more complicated.

In today's world, characterized by flatter organizations, faster innovation, and the explosion of the Internet, it is clearer than ever that to accomplish our work and meet our needs, we often have to rely on dozens, hundreds, perhaps thousands of individuals and organizations over whom we exercise no direct control. We simply cannot rely on giving orders—even when we are dealing with employees or children. To get what we want, we are compelled to negotiate. More slowly in some places, more rapidly in others, the pyramids of power are shifting into networks of negotiation. This quiet revolution, which accompanies the better-known knowledge revolution, could well be called the "negotiation revolution."

We began the first edition of *Getting to YES* with the sentence: "Like it or not, you are a negotiator." Back then, for many readers, that was an eye opener. Now it has become an acknowledged reality. Back then, the term "negotiation" was more likely to be associated with specialized activities such as labor talks, closing a sale, or perhaps international diplomacy. Now almost all of us recognize that we negotiate in an informal sense with just about everyone we meet from morning to night.

A generation ago, the term "negotiation" also had an adversarial connotation. In contemplating a negotiation, the common question in people's minds was, "Who is going to win and who is going to lose?" To reach an agreement, someone had to "give in." It was not a pleasant prospect. The idea that both sides could benefit, that both could "win," was foreign to many of us. Now it is increasingly recognized that there are cooperative ways of negotiating our differences and that even if a "win-win" solution cannot be found, a wise agreement can still often be reached that is better for both sides than the alternative.

When we were writing *Getting to YES*, very few courses taught negotiation. Now learning to negotiate well is accepted as a core competence with many courses offered in law schools, business schools, schools of government, and even in quite a few primary, elementary, and high schools.

In short, the "negotiation revolution" is now in full sway around the world, and we take heart that the commonsense tenets of principled negotiation have spread far and wide to good effect.

The work ahead

Still, while progress has been considerable, the work is far from done. Indeed, at no time in the last three decades can we recall a greater need for negotiation based on a joint search for mutual gains and legitimate standards.

A quick survey of the news on almost any day reveals the compelling need for a better way to deal with differences. How many people, organizations, and nations are stubbornly bargaining over positions? How much destructive escalation results in bitter family feuds, endless lawsuits, and wars without end? For lack of a good process, how many opportunities are being lost to find solutions that are better for both sides?

Conflict remains, as we have noted, a growth industry. Indeed, the advent of the negotiation revolution has brought more conflict, not less. Hierarchies tend to bottle up conflict, which comes out into the open as hierarchies give way to networks. Democracies surface rather than suppress conflict, which is why democracies often seem so quarrelsome and turbulent when compared with more authoritarian societies.

The goal cannot and should not be to eliminate conflict. Conflict is an inevitable—and useful—part of life. It often leads to change and generates insight. Few injustices are addressed without serious conflict. In the form of business competition, conflict helps create prosperity. And it lies at the heart of the democratic process, where the best decisions result not from a superficial consensus but from exploring different points of view and searching for creative solutions. Strange as it may seem, the world needs *more* conflict, not less.

The challenge is not to eliminate conflict but to transform it. It is to change the way we *deal* with our differences—from destructive, adversarial battling to hard-headed, side-by-side problem-solving. We should not underestimate the difficulty of this task, yet no task is more urgent in the world today.

We are living in an age that future anthropologists might look back on and call the first human family reunion. For the first time, the entire human family is in touch, thanks to the communications revolution. All fifteen thousand or so "tribes" or language communities on this planet are aware of one another around the globe. And as with many family reunions, it is not all peace and harmony, but marked by deep dissension and resentment of inequities and injustices.

More than ever, faced with the challenges of living together in a nuclear age on an increasingly crowded planet, for our own sake and the sake of future generations, we need to learn how to change the basic game of conflict.

In short, the hard work of getting to "yes" has just begun.

This edition

We have often heard from readers that *Getting to YES* continues to serve as an accessible guide to collaborative negotiation in a wide variety of fields. At the same time, we realize a younger audience is sometimes puzzled by stories and examples that were common knowledge thirty years ago, and many readers are curious about contemporary cases. So in this edition we have undertaken a careful revision and updating of examples and added some new ones where appropriate.

We have added to our toolbox considerably in thirty years, as captured in such books as *Getting Past No*, *Difficult Conversations*, *Beyond Reason*, and *The Power of a Positive No*, each of which explores important challenges in dealing collaboratively and effectively with serious differences. We've made no attempt to summarize all of that material here, since one of the virtues of *Getting to YES* is that it is short and clear. Instead, in this revision we have added a few relevant ideas where they help clarify our intent, and in other places made slight revisions to update our thinking. For example, we have made our answer to the final question in the book about negotiation power fully consistent with the "seven elements of negotiation" framework we teach at Harvard Law School.

One adjustment we considered, but ultimately rejected, was to change the word "separate" to "disentangle" in "separate the people from the problem," the powerful first step in the method of principled negotiation. Some readers have taken this phrase to mean leave aside the personal dimension of negotiation and just focus on the substantive problem, or to ignore emotional issues and "be rational." That is not our intent. Negotiators should make dealing with people issues a priority from the beginning to the end of a negotiation. As the text states at the start, "Negotiators are people first."

Our belief is that by disentangling the people from the problem you can be "soft on the people" while remaining "hard on the problem." So long as you remain respectful and attentive to people issues, you should be able to strengthen a relationship even as you disagree about substance.

Finally, we have added a bit of material on the impact of the means of communication in negotiation. The growth of email and texting and the creation of global "virtual" organizations has made this an important variable, especially in light of research showing its impact on negotiation dynamics and results.

Our human future

We are each participants in a pioneering generation of negotiators. While negotiation as a decision-making process has been around since the beginning of the human story, never has it been so central to human life and the survival of our species.

As the negotiation revolution unfolds, our aspiration is that the principles in this book continue to help people—individually and collectively—negotiate the myriad dilemmas in their lives. In the words of the poet Wallace Stevens: "After the final no there comes a yes and on that yes the future world depends."

We wish you much success in getting to that yes!

Roger Fisher
William Ury
Bruce Patton

Preface to the Second Edition

During the last ten years negotiation as a field for academic and professional concern has grown dramatically. New theoretical works have been published, case studies have been produced, and empirical research has been undertaken. Ten years ago very few professional schools offered courses on negotiation; now they are all but universal. Universities are beginning to appoint faculty who specialize in negotiation. Consulting firms now do the same in the corporate world.

Against this changing intellectual landscape, the ideas in *Getting to YES* have stood up well. They have gained considerable attention and acceptance from a broad audience and are frequently cited as starting points for other work. Happily, they remain persuasive to the authors as well. Most questions and comments have focused on areas in which the book has proven ambiguous, or where readers have wanted more specific advice. We have tried to address the most important of these topics in this revision.

Rather than tampering with the text (and asking readers who know it to search for changes), we have chosen to add new material in a separate section at the end of the second edition. The main text remains complete and unchanged from the original, except for updating the figures in examples to keep pace with inflation and rephrasing in a few places to clarify meaning and eliminate sexist language. We hope that our answers to "Ten Questions People Ask About *Getting to YES*" prove helpful and meet some of the interests readers have expressed.

We address questions about (1) the meaning and limits of "principled" negotiation (it represents practical, not moral, advice); (2) dealing with someone who seems to be irrational or who has a different value system, outlook, or negotiating style; (3) questions about tactics, such as where to meet, who should make the first offer, and how to move from inventing options to making commitments; and (4) the role of power in negotiation.

More extensive treatment of some topics will have to await other books. Readers interested in more detail about handling "people issues" in negotiation in ways that tend to establish an effective working relationship might enjoy *Getting Together: Building Relationships as We Negotiate,* by Roger Fisher and Scott Brown, also available from Penguin Books. If dealing with difficult people and situations is more your concern, look for *Getting Past No: Negotiating in Difficult Situations,* by William Ury, published by Bantam Books. No doubt other books will follow. There is certainly much more to say about power, multilateral negotiations, cross-cultural transactions, personal styles, and many other topics.

Once again we thank Marty Linsky, this time for taking a careful eye and a sharp pencil to our new material. Our special thanks to Doug Stone for his discerning critique, editing, and occasional rewriting of successive drafts of that material. He has an uncanny knack for catching us in an unclear thought or paragraph.

Roger Fisher
William Ury
Bruce Patton

For more than a dozen years, Bruce Patton has worked with us in formulating and explaining all of the ideas in this book.

This past year he has pulled the laboring oar in converting our joint thinking into an agreed text. It is a pleasure to welcome Bruce, editor of the first edition, as a full coauthor of this second edition.

R.F.
W.U.

Acknowledgments

This book began as a question: What is the best way for people to deal with their differences? For example, what is the best advice one could give a husband and wife getting divorced who want to know how to reach a fair and mutually satisfactory agreement without ending up in a bitter fight? Perhaps more difficult, what advice would you give *one* of them who wanted to do the same thing? Every day, families, neighbors, couples, employees, bosses, businesses, consumers, salesmen, lawyers, and nations face this same dilemma of how to get to yes without going to war. Drawing on our respective backgrounds in international law and anthropology and an extensive collaboration over the years with practitioners, colleagues, and students, we have evolved a practical method for negotiating agreement amicably without giving in.

We have tried out ideas on lawyers, businessmen, government officials, judges, prison wardens, diplomats, insurance representatives, military officers, coal miners, and oil executives. We gratefully acknowledge those who responded with criticism and with suggestions distilled from their experience. We benefited immensely.

In truth, so many people have contributed so extensively to our learning over the years that it is no longer possible to say precisely to whom we are indebted for which ideas in what form. Those who contributed the most understand that footnotes were omitted not because we think every idea original, but rather to keep the text readable when we owe so much to so many.

We could not fail to mention, however, our debt to Howard Raiffa. His kind but forthright criticism has repeatedly improved the approach, and his notions on seeking joint gains by exploiting differences and using imaginative procedures for settling difficult issues have inspired sections on these subjects. Louis Sohn, deviser and negotiator extraordinaire, was always encouraging, always creative, always looking forward. Among our many debts to him, we owe our introduction to the idea of using a single negotiating text, which we call the One-Text Procedure. And we would like to thank Michael Doyle and David Straus for their creative ideas on running brainstorming sessions.

Good anecdotes and examples are hard to find. We are greatly indebted to Jim Sebenius for his accounts of the Law of the Sea Conference (as well as for his thoughtful criticism of the method), to Tom Griffith for an account of his negotiation with an insurance adjuster, and to Mary Parker Follett for the story of two men quarreling in a library.

We want especially to thank all those who read this book in various drafts and gave us the benefit of their criticism, including our students in the January Negotiation Workshops of 1980 and 1981 at Harvard Law School, and Frank Sander, John Cooper, and William Lincoln, who taught those workshops with us. In particular, we want to thank those members of Harvard's Negotiation Seminar whom we have not already mentioned; they listened to us patiently these last two years and offered many helpful suggestions: John Dunlop, James Healy, David Kuechle, Thomas Schelling, and Lawrence Susskind. To all of our friends and associates we owe more than we can say, but the final responsibility for the content of this book lies with the authors; if the result is not yet perfect, it is not for lack of our colleagues' efforts.

Without family and friends, writing would be intolerable. For constructive criticism and moral support we thank Caroline Fisher,

David Lax, Frances Turnbull, and Janice Ury. Without Francis Fisher this book would never have been written. He had the felicity of introducing the two of us some four years ago.

Finer secretarial help we could not have had. Thanks to Deborah Reimel for her unfailing competence, moral support, and firm but gracious reminders, and to Denise Trybula, who never wavered in her diligence and cheerfulness. And special thanks to the people at Word Processing, led by Cynthia Smith, who met the test of an endless series of drafts and near impossible deadlines.

Then there are our editors. By reorganizing and cutting this book in half, Marty Linsky made it far more readable. To spare our readers, he had the good sense not to spare our feelings. Thanks also to Peter Kinder, June Kinoshita, and Bob Ross. June struggled to make the language less sexist. Where we have not succeeded, we apologize to those who may be offended. We also want to thank Andrea Williams, our adviser; Julian Bach, our agent; and Dick McAdoo and his associates at Houghton Mifflin, who made the production of this book both possible and pleasurable.

Finally, we want to thank Bruce Patton, our friend and colleague, editor and mediator. No one has contributed more to this book. From the very beginning he helped brainstorm and organize the syllogism of the book. He has reorganized almost every chapter and edited every word. If books were movies, this would be known as a Patton Production.

Roger Fisher
William Ury

For the second edition of this book we would like to thank Jane von Mehren, our long-time editor at Penguin Books, for her support, encouragement, and enthusiasm in making the second edition happen. With the third edition, Rick Kot has admirably filled that role and we are grateful for his patience, good sense, and fine editorial hand. Without Rick, this update might not have seen the light of day.

We also thank Mark Gordon, Arthur Martirosyan, and our friends at Mercy Corps for the account of Iraqi farmers negotiating with the national oil company.

R.F.
W.U.
B.P.

Contents

TEN QUESTIONS PEOPLE ASK ABOUT *GETTING TO YES*

QUESTIONS ABOUT FAIRNESS AND "PRINCIPLED" NEGOTIATION
Question 1: "Does positional bargaining *ever* make sense?"
Question 2: "What if the other side believes in a different standard of fairness?"
Question 3: "Should I be fair if I don't have to be?"

QUESTIONS ABOUT DEALING WITH PEOPLE
Question 4: "What do I do if the people *are* the problem?"
Question 5: "Should I negotiate even with terrorists or someone like Hitler? When does it make sense *not* to negotiate?"
Question 6: "How should I adjust my negotiating approach to account for differences of personality, gender, culture, and so on?"

QUESTIONS ABOUT TACTICS
Question 7: "How do I decide things like 'Where should we meet?' 'How should we communicate?' 'Who should make the first offer?' and 'How high should I start?'"
Question 8: "Concretely, how do I move from inventing options to making commitments?"
Question 9: "How do I try out these ideas without taking too much risk?"

QUESTIONS ABOUT POWER
Question 10: "Can the way I negotiate really make a difference if the other side is more powerful?" And "How do I enhance *my* negotiating power?"

Introduction

Like it or not, you are a negotiator. Negotiation is a fact of life. You discuss a raise with your boss. You try to agree with a stranger on a price for his house. Two lawyers try to settle a lawsuit arising from a car accident. A group of oil companies plan a joint venture exploring for offshore oil. A city official meets with union leaders to avert a transit strike. The United States Secretary of State sits down with his Russian counterpart to seek an agreement limiting nuclear arms. All these are negotiations.

Everyone negotiates something every day. Like Molière's Monsieur Jourdain, who was delighted to learn that he had been speaking prose all his life, people negotiate even when they don't think of themselves as doing so. You negotiate with your spouse about where to go for dinner and with your child about when the lights go out. Negotiation is a basic means of getting what you want from others. It is back-and-forth communication designed to reach an agreement when you and the other side have some interests that are shared and others that are opposed (as well as some that may simply be different).

More and more occasions require negotiation; conflict is a growth industry. Everyone wants to participate in decisions that affect them; fewer and fewer people will accept decisions dictated by someone else. People differ, and they use negotiation to handle their differences. Whether in business, government, or the family, people reach most decisions through negotiation. Even when they go to court, they almost always negotiate a settlement before trial.

Although negotiation takes place every day, it is not easy to do well. Standard strategies for negotiation often leave people dissatisfied, worn out, or alienated—and frequently all three.

People find themselves in a dilemma. They see two ways to negotiate: soft or hard. The soft negotiator wants to avoid personal conflict and so makes concessions readily to reach agreement. He or she wants an amicable resolution; yet often ends up exploited and feeling bitter. The hard negotiator sees any situation as a contest of wills in which the side that takes the more extreme positions and holds out longer fares better. He or she wants to win; yet often ends up producing an equally hard response that exhausts the negotiator and his or her resources and harms the relationship with the other side. Other standard negotiating strategies fall between hard and soft, but each involves an attempted trade-off between getting what you want and getting along with people.

There is a third way to negotiate, a way neither hard nor soft, but rather both hard *and* soft. The method of *principled negotiation* developed at the Harvard Negotiation Project is to decide issues on their merits rather than through a haggling process focused on what each side says it will and won't do. It suggests that you look for mutual gains whenever possible, and that where your interests conflict, you should insist that the result be based on some fair standards independent of the will of either side. The method of principled negotiation is hard on the merits, soft on the people. It employs no tricks and no posturing. Principled negotiation shows you how to obtain what you are entitled to and still be decent. It enables you to be fair while protecting you against those who would take advantage of your fairness.

This book is about the method of principled negotiation. The first chapter describes problems that arise in using the standard strategies of positional bargaining. The next four chapters lay out the four principles of the method. The last three chapters answer the questions most commonly asked about the method: What if the other side is more powerful? What if they will not play along? And what if they use dirty tricks?

Principled negotiation can be used by diplomats in arms control talks, investment bankers negotiating corporate acquisitions, and by couples in deciding everything from where to go for vacation to how to divide their property if they get divorced. It is even a staple of hostage negotiators seeking the release of kidnap victims. Anyone can use this method.

Every negotiation is different, but the basic elements do not change. Principled negotiation can be used whether there is one issue or several; two parties or many; whether there is a prescribed ritual, as in collective bargaining, or an impromptu free-for-all, as in talking with hijackers. The method applies whether the other side is more experienced or less, a hard bargainer or a friendly one. Principled negotiation is an all-purpose strategy. Unlike almost all other strategies, if the other side learns this one, it does not become more difficult to use; it becomes easier. If they read this book, all the better.

Getting to
YES

I THE PROBLEM

1 Don't Bargain Over Positions

Whether a negotiation concerns a contract, a family quarrel, or a peace settlement among nations, people routinely engage in positional bargaining. Each side takes a position, argues for it, and makes concessions to reach a compromise. The classic example of this negotiating minuet is the haggling that takes place between a customer and the proprietor of a secondhand store:

Customer	Shopkeeper
How much do you want for this brass dish?	
	That is a beautiful antique, isn't it? I guess I could let it go for $75.
Oh come on, it's dented. I'll give you $15.	
	Really! I might consider a serious offer, but $15 certainly isn't serious.
Well, I could go to $20, but I would never pay anything like $75. Quote me a realistic price.	
	You drive a hard bargain, young lady. $60 cash, right now.
$25.	
	It cost me a great deal more than that. Make me a *serious* offer.

Customer	**Shopkeeper**
$37.50. That's the highest I will go.	Have you noticed the engraving on that dish? Next year pieces like that will be worth twice what you pay today.

And so it goes, on and on. Perhaps they will reach agreement; perhaps not.

Any method of negotiation may be fairly judged by three criteria: It should produce a wise agreement if agreement is possible. It should be efficient. And it should improve or at least not damage the relationship between the parties. (A wise agreement can be defined as one that meets the legitimate interests of each side to the extent possible, resolves conflicting interests fairly, is durable, and takes community interests into account.)

The most common form of negotiation, illustrated by the above example, depends upon successively taking—and then giving up—a sequence of positions.

Taking positions, as the customer and storekeeper do, serves some useful purposes in a negotiation. It tells the other side what you want; it provides an anchor in an uncertain and pressured situation; and it can eventually produce the terms of an acceptable agreement. But those purposes can be served in other ways. And positional bargaining fails to meet the basic criteria of producing a wise agreement, efficiently and amicably.

Arguing over positions produces unwise outcomes

When negotiators bargain over positions, they tend to lock themselves into those positions. The more you clarify your position and defend it against attack, the more committed you become to it. The more you try to convince the other side of the impossibility of changing your opening position, the more difficult it becomes to do so. Your ego becomes identified with your position. You now have a new interest in "saving face"—in reconciling future action with past positions—making it less and less likely that any agreement will wisely reconcile the parties' original interests.

The danger that positional bargaining will impede a negotiation was well illustrated in 1961 by the breakdown of the talks under President John F. Kennedy for a comprehensive ban on nuclear testing, which, if enacted, might have headed off much of the superpower arms race that ensued over the next three decades. A critical question arose: How many on-site inspections per year should the Soviet Union and the United States be permitted to make within the other's territory to investigate suspicious seismic events? The Soviet Union finally agreed to three inspections. The United States insisted on no less than ten. And there the talks broke down—over positions—despite the fact that no one understood whether an "inspection" would involve one person looking around for one day, or a hundred people prying indiscriminately for a month. The parties had made little attempt to design an inspection procedure that would reconcile the United States's interest in verification with the desire of both countries for minimal intrusion.

Focusing on positions nearly led to unnecessary bloodshed in a dispute between farmers and the national oil company in Iraq after the fall of the Saddam Hussein regime. Displaced farmers in the south of Iraq had banded together, leased arable land from the government, and used their last savings and borrowings to plant crops. Unfortunately, only a few months later the farmers received a letter calling for them to vacate the land immediately in accord with the fine print of their lease, because oil had been discovered under it. The oil company said, "Get off our land." The farmers replied, "It's our land, and we're not leaving." The oil company threatened to call the police. The farmers said, "There are more of us," so the national oil company threatened to bring in the army. "We have guns too; we aren't leaving," came the reply. "We have nothing left to lose."

As troops gathered, bloodshed was averted only by the last-minute intervention of an official fresh from a training program in alternatives to positional bargaining. "How long will it be before you expect to produce oil on this land?" he asked the national oil company. "Probably three years," they replied. "What do you plan to do on the land over the next few months?" "Mapping; a little seismic surveying of the underground layers." Then he asked the farmers, "What's the problem with leaving now, as they've asked?" "The harvest is in six weeks. It represents everything we own."

Shortly thereafter an agreement was reached: The farmers could harvest their crops. They would not impede the oil company's preparatory activities. Indeed, the oil company hoped soon to hire many of the farmers as laborers for its construction activities. And it did not object if they continued to plant crops in between oil derricks.

As illustrated in these examples, the more attention that is paid to positions, the less attention is devoted to meeting the underlying concerns of the parties. Agreement becomes less likely. Any agreement reached may reflect a mechanical splitting of the difference between final positions rather than a solution carefully crafted to meet the legitimate interests of the parties. The result is frequently an agreement less satisfactory to each side than it could have been, or no agreement at all, when a good agreement was possible.

Arguing over positions is inefficient

The standard method of negotiation may produce either agreement, as with the price of a brass dish, or breakdown, as with the number of on-site inspections. In either event, the process takes a lot of time.

Bargaining over positions creates incentives that stall settlement. In positional bargaining you try to improve the chance that any settlement reached is favorable to you by starting with an extreme position, by stubbornly holding to it, by deceiving the other party as to your true views, and by making small concessions only as necessary to keep the negotiation going. The same is true for the other side. Each of those factors tends to interfere with reaching a settlement promptly. The more extreme the opening positions and the smaller the concessions, the more time and effort it will take to discover whether or not agreement is possible.

The standard minuet also requires a large number of individual decisions as each negotiator decides what to offer, what to reject, and how much of a concession to make. Decision-making is difficult and time-consuming at best. Where each decision not only involves yielding to the other side but will likely produce pressure to yield further, a negotiator has little incentive to move quickly. Dragging one's feet, threatening to walk out, stonewalling, and other such tactics become commonplace. They all increase the time and costs of reaching agreement as well as the risk that no agreement will be reached at all.

Arguing over positions endangers an ongoing relationship

Positional bargaining becomes a contest of will. Each negotiator asserts what he will and won't do. The task of jointly devising an acceptable solution tends to become a battle. Each side tries through sheer willpower to force the other to change its position. "I'm not going to give in. If you want to go to the movies with me, it's *Avatar* or nothing." Anger and resentment often result as one side sees itself bending to the rigid will of the other while its own legitimate concerns go unaddressed. Positional bargaining thus strains and sometimes shatters the relationship between the parties. Commercial enterprises that have been doing business together for years may part company. Neighbors may stop speaking to each other. Bitter feelings generated by one such encounter may last a lifetime.

When there are many parties, positional bargaining is even worse

Although it is convenient to discuss negotiation in terms of two persons, you and "the other side," in fact, almost every negotiation involves more than two persons. Several different parties may sit at the table, or each side may have constituents, higher-ups, boards of directors, or committees with whom they must deal. The more people involved in a negotiation, the more serious the drawbacks to positional bargaining.

If some 150 countries are negotiating, as in various United Nations conferences, positional bargaining is next to impossible. It may take all to say yes, but only one to say no. Reciprocal concessions are difficult: to whom do you make a concession? Yet even thousands of bilateral deals would still fall short of a multilateral agreement. In such situations, positional bargaining leads to the formation of coalitions among parties whose shared interests are often more symbolic than substantive. At the United Nations, such coalitions often produce negotiations between "the" North and "the" South, or between "the" East and "the" West. Because there are many members in a group, it becomes more difficult to develop a common position. What is worse, once they have painfully developed and agreed upon a position, it becomes much harder to change it. Altering a position proves equally difficult when additional participants are higher authorities who, while absent from the table, must nevertheless give their approval.

Being nice is no answer

Many people recognize the high costs of hard positional bargaining, particularly on the parties and their relationship. They hope to avoid them by following a more gentle style of negotiation. Instead of seeing the other side as adversaries, they prefer to see them as friends. Rather than emphasizing a goal of victory, they emphasize the necessity of reaching agreement. In a soft negotiating game the standard moves are to make offers and concessions, to trust the other side, to be friendly, and to yield as necessary to avoid confrontation.

The following table illustrates two styles of positional bargaining, soft and hard. Most people see their choice of negotiating strategies as between these two styles. Looking at the table as presenting a choice, should you be a soft or a hard positional bargainer? Or should you perhaps follow a strategy somewhere in between?

The soft negotiating game emphasizes the importance of building and maintaining a relationship. Within families and among friends much negotiation takes place in this way. The process tends to be efficient, at least to the extent of producing results quickly. As each party competes with the other in being more generous

Problem	
Positional Bargaining: Which Game Should You Play?	
Soft	**Hard**
Participants are friends.	Participants are adversaries.
The goal is agreement.	The goal is victory.
Make concessions to cultivate the relationship.	Demand concessions as a condition of the relationship.
Be soft on the people and the problem.	Be hard on the problem and the people.
Trust others.	Distrust others.
Change your position easily.	Dig in to your position.
Make *offers*.	Make threats.
Disclose your bottom line.	Mislead as to your bottom line.
Accept one-sided losses to reach agreement.	Demand one-sided gains as the price of agreement.
Search for the single answer: the one *they* will accept.	Search for the single answer: the one *you* will accept.
Insist on agreement.	Insist on your position.
Try to avoid a contest of will.	Try to win a contest of will.
Yield to pressure.	Apply pressure.

and more forthcoming, an agreement becomes highly likely. But it may not be a wise one. The results may not be as tragic as in the O. Henry story about an impoverished couple in which the loving wife sells her hair in order to buy a handsome chain for her husband's watch, and the unknowing husband sells his watch in order to buy beautiful combs for his wife's hair. However, any negotiation primarily concerned with the relationship runs the risk of producing a sloppy agreement.

More seriously, pursuing a soft and friendly form of positional bargaining makes you vulnerable to someone who plays a hard game of positional bargaining. In positional bargaining, a hard game dominates a soft one. If the hard bargainer insists on concessions and makes threats while the soft bargainer yields in order to avoid confrontation and insists on agreement, the negotiating game is biased in favor of the hard player. The process will produce an agreement, although it may not be a wise one. It will certainly be more favorable to the hard positional bargainer than to the soft one. If your response to sustained, hard positional bargaining is soft positional bargaining, you will probably lose your shirt.

There is an alternative

If you do not like the choice between hard and soft positional bargaining, you can change the game.

The game of negotiation takes place at two levels. At one level, negotiation addresses the substance; at another, it focuses— usually implicitly—on the procedure for dealing with the substance. The first negotiation may concern your salary, the terms of a lease, or a price to be paid. The second negotiation concerns how you will negotiate the substantive question: by soft positional bargaining, by hard positional bargaining, or by some other method. This second negotiation is a game about a game—a "meta-game." Each move you make within a negotiation is not only a move that deals with rent, salary, or other substantive questions; it also helps structure the rules of the game you are playing. Your move may serve to keep the negotiations within an ongoing mode, or it may constitute a game-changing move.

This second negotiation by and large escapes notice because it seems to occur without conscious decision. Only when dealing with someone from another country, particularly someone with a markedly different cultural background, are you likely to see the necessity of establishing some accepted process for the substantive negotiations. But whether consciously or not, you are negotiating procedural rules with every move you make, even if those moves appear exclusively concerned with substance.

The answer to the question of whether to use soft positional bargaining or hard is "neither." Change the game. At the Harvard Negotiation Project we have been developing an alternative to positional bargaining: a method of negotiation explicitly designed to produce wise outcomes efficiently and amicably. This method, called *principled negotiation* or *negotiation on the merits,* can be boiled down to four basic points.

These four points define a straightforward method of negotiation that can be used under almost any circumstance. Each point deals with a basic element of negotiation, and suggests what you should do about it.

People:	Separate the people from the problem.
Interests:	Focus on interests, not positions.
Options:	Invent multiple options looking for mutual gains before deciding what to do.
Criteria:	Insist that the result be based on some objective standard.

The method of principled negotiation is contrasted with hard and soft positional bargaining in the table below, which shows the four basic points of the method in boldface type.

The first point responds to the fact that human beings are not computers. We are creatures of strong emotions who often have radically different perceptions and have difficulty communicating clearly. Emotions typically become entangled with the objective merits of the problem. Taking positions just makes this worse because people's egos become identified with their positions. Making concessions "for the relationship" is equally problematic, because it can actually encourage and reward stubbornness, which can lead to resentment that ends up damaging the relationship. Hence, even before working on the substantive problem, the "people problem" should be disentangled from it and addressed on its own. Figuratively if not literally, the participants should come to see themselves as working side by side, attacking the problem, not each other. Hence the first proposition: *Separate the people from the problem.*

The second point is designed to overcome the drawback of focusing on people's stated positions when the object of a negotiation is to satisfy their underlying interests. A negotiating position often obscures what you really want. Compromising between positions is not likely to produce an agreement that will effectively take care of the human needs that led people to adopt those positions. The second basic element of the method is: *Focus on interests, not positions.*

The third point responds to the difficulty of designing optimal solutions while under pressure. Trying to decide in the presence of an adversary narrows your vision. Having a lot at stake inhibits creativity. So does searching for the one right solution. You can offset these constraints by setting aside a designated time within which to think up a wide range of possible solutions that advance shared interests and creatively reconcile differing interests. Hence the third basic point: Before trying to reach agreement, *invent options for mutual gain.*

Where interests are directly opposed, a negotiator may be able to obtain a favorable result simply by being stubborn. That method tends to reward intransigence and produce arbitrary results. However, you can counter such a negotiator by insisting that his single say-so is not enough and that the agreement must reflect some fair standard independent of the naked will of either

Problem Positional Bargaining: Which Game Should You Play?		**Solution** Change the Game— Negotiate on the Merits
Soft	**Hard**	**Principled**
Participants are friends.	Participants are adversaries.	Participants are problem-solvers.
The goal is agreement.	The goal is victory.	The goal is a wise outcome reached efficiently and amicably.
Make concessions to cultivate the relationship.	Demand concessions as a condition of the relationship.	**Separate the people from the problem.**
Be soft on the people and the problem.	Be hard on the problem and the people.	Be soft on the people, hard on the problem.
Trust others.	Distrust others.	Proceed independent of trust.
Change your position easily.	Dig in to your position.	**Focus on interests, not positions.**
Make offers.	Make threats.	Explore interests.
Disclose your bottom line.	Mislead as to your bottom line.	Avoid having a bottom line.
Accept one-sided losses to reach agreement.	Demand one-sided gains as the price of agreement.	**Invent options for mutual gain.**
Search for the single answer: the one *they* will accept.	Search for the single answer: the one *you* will accept.	Develop multiple options to choose from; decide later.
Insist on agreement.	Insist on your position.	**Insist on using objective criteria.**
Try to avoid a contest of will.	Try to win a contest of will.	Try to reach a result based on standards independent of will.
Yield to pressure.	Apply pressure.	Reason and be open to reason; yield to principle, not pressure.

side. This does not mean insisting that the terms be based on the standard you select, but only that some fair standard such as market value, expert opinion, custom, or law determine the outcome. By discussing such criteria rather than what the parties are willing or unwilling to do, neither party need give in to the other; both can defer to a fair solution. Hence the fourth basic point: *Insist on using objective criteria.*

The four propositions of principled negotiation are relevant from the time you begin to think about negotiating until the time either an agreement is reached or you decide to break off the effort. That period can be divided into three stages: analysis, planning, and discussion.

During the *analysis* stage you are simply trying to diagnose the situation—to gather information, organize it, and think about it. You will want to consider the people problems of partisan perceptions, hostile emotions, and unclear communication, as well as to identify your interests and those of the other side. You will want to note options already on the table and identify any criteria already suggested as a basis for agreement.

During the *planning* stage you deal with the same four elements a second time, both generating ideas and deciding what to do. How do you propose to handle the people problems? Of your interests, which are most important? And what are some realistic objectives? You will want to generate additional options and additional criteria for deciding among them.

Again during the *discussion* stage, when the parties communicate back and forth, looking toward agreement, the same four elements are the best subjects to discuss. Differences in perception, feelings of frustration and anger, and difficulties in communication can be acknowledged and addressed. Each side should come to understand the interests of the other. Both can then jointly generate options that are mutually advantageous and seek agreement on objective standards for resolving opposed interests.

To sum up, in contrast to positional bargaining, the principled negotiation method of focusing on basic interests, mutually satisfying options, and fair standards typically results in a *wise* agreement. The method permits you to reach a gradual consensus on a joint decision *efficiently* without all the transactional costs of digging in to positions only to have to dig yourself out of them. And separating the people from the problem allows you to deal directly and empathetically with the other negotiator as a human being regardless of any substantive differences, thus making possible an *amicable* outcome.

Each of the next four chapters expands on one of these four basic points. If at any point you become skeptical, you may want to skip ahead briefly and browse in chapters six, seven, and eight, which respond to questions commonly raised about the method.

II THE METHOD

2. Separate the **People** from the Problem
3. Focus on **Interests,** Not Positions
4. Invent **Options** for Mutual Gain
5. Insist on Using Objective **Criteria**

2 Separate the People from the Problem

Everyone knows how hard it is to deal with a problem without people misunderstanding each other, getting angry or upset, and taking things personally.

A union leader says to his crew, "All right, who called the walkout?"

Jones steps forward. "I did. It was that bum foreman Campbell again. That was the fifth time in two weeks he sent me out of our group as a replacement. He's got it in for me, and I'm tired of it. Why should I get all the dirty work?"

Later the union leader confronts Campbell. "Why do you keep picking on Jones? He says you've put him on replacement detail five times in two weeks. What's going on?"

Campbell replies, "I pick Jones because he's the best. I know I can trust him to keep things from fouling up in a group without its point person. I send him on replacement only when it's a key person missing, otherwise I send Smith or someone else. It's just that with the flu going around there've been a lot of point people out. I never knew Jones objected. I thought he liked the responsibility."

In another real-life situation, an insurance company lawyer says to the state insurance commissioner:

"I appreciate your time, Commissioner Thompson. What I'd like to talk to you about is some of the problems we've been having with the presumption clause of the strict-liability regulations. Basically, we think the way the clause was written causes it to have an unfair impact on those insurers whose existing policies contain rate adjustment limitations, and we would like to consider ways it might be revised—"

The Commissioner, interrupting: "Ms. Monteiro, your company had ample opportunity to voice any objection it had during the hearings my department held on those regulations before they were issued. I ran those hearings, Ms. Monteiro. I listened to every word of testimony, and I wrote the final version of the strict-liability provisions personally. Are you saying I made a mistake?"

"No, but—"

"Are you saying I'm unfair?"

"Certainly not, sir, but I think this provision has had consequences none of us foresaw, and—"

"Listen, Monteiro, I promised the public when I campaigned for this position that I would put an end to killer hair dryers and $10,000 bombs disguised as cars. And these regulations have done that.

"Your company made a $50 million profit on its strict-liability policies last year. What kind of fool do you think you can play me for, coming in here talking about 'unfair' regulations and 'unforeseen consequences'? I don't want to hear another word of that. Good day, Ms. Monteiro."

Now what? Does the insurance company lawyer press the Commissioner on this point, making him angry and probably not getting anywhere? Her company does a lot of business in this state. A good relationship with the Commissioner is important. Should she let the matter rest, then, even though she is convinced that this regulation really is unfair, that its long-term effects are likely to be against the public interest, and that not even the experts foresaw this problem at the time of the original hearings?

What is going on in these cases?

Negotiators are people first

A basic fact about negotiation, easy to forget in corporate and international transactions, is that you are dealing not with abstract representatives of the "other side," but with human beings. They have emotions, deeply held values, and different backgrounds and viewpoints; and they are unpredictable. They are prone to cognitive biases, partisan perceptions, blind spots, and leaps of illogic. So are we.

This human aspect of negotiation can be either helpful or disastrous. The process of working out an agreement may produce a psychological commitment to a mutually satisfactory outcome. A working relationship where trust, understanding, respect, and friendship are built up over time can make each new negotiation smoother and more efficient. And people's desire to feel good about themselves, and their concern for what others will think of them, can often make them more sensitive to another negotiator's interests.

On the other hand, people get angry, depressed, fearful, hostile, frustrated, and offended. They have egos that are easily threatened. They see the world from their own personal vantage point, and they frequently confuse their perceptions with reality. Routinely, they fail to interpret what you say in the way you intend and do not mean what you understand them to say. Misunderstanding can reinforce prejudice and lead to reactions that produce counterreactions in a vicious circle; rational exploration of possible solutions becomes impossible and a negotiation fails. The purpose of the game becomes scoring points, confirming negative impressions, and apportioning blame at the expense of the substantive interests of both parties.

Failing to deal with others sensitively as human beings prone to human reactions can be disastrous for a negotiation. Whatever else you are doing at any point during a negotiation, from preparation to follow-up, it is worth asking yourself, "Am I paying enough attention to the people problem?"

Every negotiator has two kinds of interests: in the substance and in the relationship

Every negotiator wants to reach an agreement that satisfies his substantive interests. That is why one negotiates. Beyond that, a negotiator also has an interest in his relationship with the other side. An antiques dealer wants both to make a profit on the sale and to turn the customer into a regular one. At a minimum, a negotiator wants to maintain a working relationship good enough to produce an acceptable agreement (and effective implementation) if one is possible given each side's interests. Usually, more is at stake. Most negotiations take place in the context of an ongoing relationship where it is important to carry on each negotiation in a way that will help rather than hinder future relations and future negotiations. In fact, with many long-term clients, business partners, family members, fellow professionals, government officials, or foreign nations, the ongoing relationship is far more important than the outcome of any particular negotiation.

The relationship tends to become entangled with the problem. A major consequence of the "people problem" in negotiation is that the parties' relationship tends to become entangled with their discussions of substance. On both the giving and receiving end, we are likely to treat people and problem as one. Within the family, a statement such as "The kitchen is a mess" or "Our bank account is *low*" may be intended simply to identify a problem, but it is likely to be heard as a personal attack. Anger over a situation may lead you to express anger toward some human being associated with it in your mind. Egos tend to become involved in substantive positions.

Another reason that substantive issues become entangled with psychological ones is that people draw from comments on substance unfounded inferences, which they then treat as facts about that person's intentions and attitudes toward them. Unless we are careful, this process is almost automatic; we are seldom aware that other explanations may be equally valid. Thus in the union example, Jones was sure that Campbell, the foreman, had it in for him, while Campbell thought it obvious that he was complimenting Jones and doing him a favor by giving him responsible assignments.

Positional bargaining puts relationship and substance in

conflict. Framing a negotiation as a contest of will over positions aggravates the entangling process. I see your position as a statement of how you would like the negotiation to end; from my point of view it demonstrates how little you care about our relationship. If I take a firm position that you consider unreasonable, you assume that I also think of it as an extreme position; it is easy to conclude that I do not value our relationship—or you— very highly.

Positional bargaining deals with a negotiator's interests both in substance and in a good relationship by trading one off against the other. If what counts in the long run for your company is its relationship with the insurance commissioner, then you will probably let this matter drop. Yet giving in on a substantive point may buy no friendship; it may do nothing more than convince the other side that you can be taken for a ride. Or, if you care more about a favorable solution than being respected or liked by the other side, you can try to extract concessions by holding the relationship hostage. "If you won't go along with me on this point, then so much for you. This will be the last time we meet." While you *may* extract a concession this way, this strategy often results in lousy substance *and* a damaged relationship.

Disentangle the relationship from the substance; deal directly with the people problem

Dealing with a substantive problem and maintaining a good working relationship need not be conflicting goals if the parties are committed and psychologically prepared to treat each separately on its own legitimate merits. Base the relationship on mutually understood perceptions, clear two-way communication, expressing emotions without blame, and a forward-looking, purposive outlook. Deal with people problems by changing how you treat people; don't try to solve them with substantive concessions.

To deal with psychological problems, use psychological techniques. Where perceptions differ, look for ways to test assumptions and to educate. If emotions run high, you can find ways for each person involved to let off steam and feel heard. Where misunderstanding exists, you can work to improve communication.

To find your way through the jungle of people problems, it is useful to think in terms of three basic categories: perception, emotion, and communication. The various people problems all fall into one of these three baskets.

In negotiating it is easy to forget that you must deal not only with their people problems, but also with your own. Your anger and frustration may obstruct an agreement beneficial to you. Your perceptions are likely to be one-sided, and you may not be listening or communicating adequately. The techniques that follow apply equally well to your people problems as to those of the other side.

Perception

Understanding the other side's thinking is not simply a useful activity that will help you solve your problem. Their thinking *is* the problem. Whether you are making a deal or settling a dispute, differences are defined by the difference between your thinking and theirs. When two people quarrel, they usually quarrel over an object — both may claim a watch — or over an event — each may contend that the other was at fault in causing an automobile accident. The same goes for nations. Morocco and Algeria quarrel over a section of the Western Sahara; India and Pakistan quarrel over each other's development of nuclear bombs. In such circumstances people tend to assume that what they need to know more about is the object or the event. They study the watch or they measure the skid marks at the scene of the accident. They study the Western Sahara or the detailed history of nuclear weapons development in India and Pakistan.

Ultimately, however, conflict lies not in objective reality, but in people's heads. Truth is simply one more argument — perhaps a good one, perhaps not — for dealing with the difference. The difference itself exists because it exists in their thinking. Fears, even if ill-founded, are real fears and need to be dealt with. Hopes, even if unrealistic, may cause a war. Facts, even if established, may do nothing to solve the problem. Both parties may agree that one lost the watch and the other found it, but still disagree over who should get it. It may finally be established that the auto accident was caused by the blowout of a tire that had been driven 31,402 miles, but the parties may dispute who should pay for the damage. The detailed history and geography of the Western Sahara, no matter how carefully studied and documented, is not the stuff with which one puts to rest that kind of territorial dispute. No study of who developed what nuclear devices when will put to rest the conflict between India and Pakistan.

As useful as looking for objective reality can be, it is ultimately the reality as each side sees it that constitutes the problem in a negotiation and opens the way to a solution.

Put yourself in their shoes. How you see the world depends on where you sit. People tend to see what they want to see. Out of a mass of detailed information, they tend to pick out and focus on those facts that confirm their prior perceptions and to disregard or misinterpret those that call their perceptions into question. Each side in a negotiation may see only the merits of its case, and only the faults of the other side's.

The ability to see the situation as the other side sees it, as difficult as it may be, is one of the most important skills a negotiator can possess. It is not enough to know that they see things differently. If you want to influence them, you also need to understand empathetically the power of their point of view and to feel the emotional force with which they believe in it. It is not enough to study them like beetles under a microscope; you need to know what it feels like to be a beetle. To accomplish this task you should be prepared to withhold judgment for a while as you "try on" their views. They may well believe that their views are "right" as strongly as you believe yours are. You may see on the table a glass half full of cool water. Your spouse may see a dirty, half-empty glass about to cause a ring on the mahogany finish.

Tenant's perceptions	Landlady's perceptions
The rent is already too high.	The rent has not been increased for a long time.
With other costs going up, I can't afford to pay more for housing.	With other costs going up, I need more rental income.
The apartment needs painting.	He has given that apartment heavy wear and tear.
I know people who pay less for a comparable apartment.	I know people who pay more for a comparable apartment.
Young people like me can't afford to pay high rents.	Young people like him tend to make noise and to be hard on an apartment.
The rent ought to be low because the neighborhood is rundown.	We landlords should raise rents to improve the quality of the neighborhood.
I am a desirable tenant with no dogs or cats.	His loud music drives me crazy.
I always pay the rent whenever she asks for it.	He never pays the rent until I ask for it.
She is cold and distant; she never asks me how things are.	I am a considerate person who never intrudes on a tenant's privacy.

Consider the contrasting perceptions of a tenant and a landlady negotiating the renewal of a lease:

Understanding their point of view is not the same as agreeing with it. It is true that a better understanding of their thinking may lead you to revise your own views about the merits of a situation. But that is not a *cost* of understanding their point of view, it is a *benefit*. It allows you to reduce the area of conflict, and it also helps you advance your newly enlightened self-interest.

Don't deduce their intentions from your fears. People tend to assume that whatever they fear, the other side intends to do. Consider this story from the *New York Times:* "They met in a bar, where he offered her a ride home. He took her down unfamiliar streets. He said it was a shortcut. He got her home so fast she caught the ten o'clock news." Why is the ending so surprising? We made an assumption based on our fears.

It is all too easy to fall into the habit of putting the worst interpretation on what the other side says or does. A suspicious interpretation often follows naturally from one's existing perceptions. Moreover, it seems the "safe" thing to do, and it shows spectators how bad the other side really is. But the cost of interpreting whatever they say or do in its most dismal light is that fresh ideas in the direction of agreement are spurned, and subtle changes of position are ignored or rejected.

Don't blame them for your problem. It is tempting to hold the other side responsible for your problem. "Your company is totally unreliable. Every time you service our rotary generator here at the factory, you do a lousy job and it breaks down again." Blaming is an easy mode to fall into, particularly when you feel that the other side is indeed responsible. But even if blaming is justified, it is usually counterproductive. Under attack, the other side will become defensive and will resist what you have to say. They will cease to listen, or they will strike back with an attack of their own. Assessing blame firmly entangles the people with the problem.

When you talk about the problem, distinguish the symptoms from the person with whom you are talking. "Our rotary generator that you service has broken down again. That is three times in the last month. The first time it was out of order for an entire week. This factory needs a functioning generator. I need your advice on how we can minimize our risk of generator breakdown. Should we change service companies, sue the manufacturer, or what?"

Discuss each other's perceptions. One way to deal with differing perceptions is to make them explicit and discuss them with the other side. As long as you do this in a frank, honest manner without either side blaming the other for the problem as each sees it, such a discussion may provide the understanding they need to take what you say seriously, and vice versa.

It is common in a negotiation to treat as "unimportant" those concerns of the other side perceived as not standing in the way of an agreement. To the contrary, communicating loudly and convincingly things you are willing to say that they would like to hear can be one of the best investments you as a negotiator can make.

Consider the negotiation over the transfer of technology that arose at the multinational Law of the Sea Conference. From 1974 to 1981 representatives of some 150 nations gathered in New York and Geneva to formulate rules to govern uses of the ocean from fishing rights to mining manganese in the deep seabed. At one point, representatives of the developing countries expressed keen interest in an exchange of technology; their countries wanted to be able to acquire from the highly industrialized nations advanced technical knowledge and equipment for deep-seabed mining.

The United States and other developed countries saw no difficulty in satisfying that desire—and therefore saw the issue of technology transfer as unimportant. In one sense it was unimportant to them, but it was a great mistake for them to *treat* the subject as unimportant. By devoting substantial time to working out the practical arrangements for transferring technology, they might have made their offer far more credible and far more attractive to the developing countries. By dismissing the issue as a matter of lesser importance to be dealt with later, the industrialized states gave up a low-cost opportunity to provide the developing countries with an impressive achievement and a real incentive to reach agreement on other issues.

Look for opportunities to act inconsistently with their perceptions. Perhaps the best way to change someone's perceptions is to send them a message different from what they expect. The visit of Egypt's President Anwar Sadat to Jerusalem in November 1977 provides an outstanding example of such an action. At the time, Israelis saw Sadat and Egypt as their enemy, the man and country that had launched a surprise attack on them four years before. To alter that perception, to help persuade the Israelis that he too desired peace, Sadat flew to the capital of his enemies, a disputed capital that not even the United States, Israel's best friend, had recognized as the capital of Israel. Instead of acting as an enemy, Sadat acted as a partner. Without this dramatic move, it is hard to imagine the signing of an Egyptian-Israeli peace treaty in 1979.

Give them a stake in the outcome by making sure they participate in the process. If they are not involved in the process, they are unlikely to approve the product. It is that simple. If you go to the state insurance commissioner prepared for battle after a long investigation, it is not surprising that he is going to feel threatened and resist your conclusions. If you fail to ask an employee whether he wants an assignment with responsibility, don't be surprised to find out that he resents it. If you want the other side to accept a disagreeable conclusion, it is crucial that you involve them in the process of reaching that conclusion.

This is precisely what people tend not to do. When you have a difficult issue to handle, your instinct is to leave the hard part until last. "Let's be sure we have the whole thing worked out before we approach the Commissioner." The Commissioner, however, is much more likely to agree to a revision of the regulations if he feels that he has had a part in drafting it. This way the revision becomes just one more small step in the long drafting process that produced his original regulation rather than someone's attempt to butcher his completed product.

During the nearly fifty-year struggle against apartheid (legalized racial segregation) in South Africa that ended only with the multiparty elections of 1994, white moderates at one point were trying to abolish the discriminatory pass laws. How? By meeting in an all-white parliamentary committee to discuss proposals. Yet however meritorious those proposals might prove, they would be insufficient, not necessarily because of their substance, but because they would be the product of a process in which no blacks were included. Blacks would hear, "We superior whites are going to figure out how to solve your problems." It would be the "white man's burden" all over again, which was the problem to start with.

Even if the terms of an agreement seem favorable, the other side may reject them simply out of a suspicion born of their exclusion from the drafting process. Agreement becomes much easier if both parties feel ownership of the ideas. The whole process of negotiation becomes stronger as each side puts their imprimatur bit by bit on a developing solution. Each criticism of the terms and consequent change, each compromise, is a personal mark that the negotiator leaves on a proposal. A proposal evolves that bears enough of the suggestions of both sides for each to feel it is theirs.

To give the other side a feeling of participation, get them involved early. Ask their advice. Giving credit generously for ideas wherever possible will give them a personal stake in defending those ideas to others. It may be hard to resist the temptation to take credit for yourself, but forbearance pays off handsomely. Apart from the substantive merits, the feeling of participation in the process is perhaps the single most important factor in determining whether a negotiator accepts a proposal. In a sense, the process *is* the product.

Face-saving: Make your proposals consistent with their values. In the English language, "face-saving" carries a derogatory flavor. People say, "We are doing that just to let them save face," implying that a little pretense has been created to allow someone to go along without feeling badly. The tone implies ridicule.

This is a grave misunderstanding of the role and importance of face-saving. Face-saving reflects people's need to reconcile the stand taken in a negotiation or an agreement with their existing principles and with their past words and deeds.

The judicial process concerns itself with the same subject. When a judge writes an opinion on a court ruling, she is saving face, not only for herself and for the judicial system, but for the parties. Instead of just telling one party, "You win," and telling the other, "You lose," she explains how her decision is consistent with principle, law, and precedent. She wants to appear not as arbitrary, but as behaving in a proper fashion. A negotiator is no different.

Often in a negotiation people will continue to hold out not because the proposal on the table is inherently unacceptable, but simply because they want to avoid the feeling or the appearance of backing down to the other side. If the substance can be phrased or conceptualized differently so that it seems a fair outcome, they will then accept it. Terms negotiated between a major city and its Hispanic community on access to municipal jobs were unacceptable to the mayor — until the agreement was withdrawn and the mayor was allowed to announce the same terms as his own decision, carrying out a campaign promise.

Face-saving involves reconciling an agreement with principle and with the self-image of the negotiators. Its importance should not be underestimated.

Emotion

In a negotiation, particularly in a bitter dispute, feelings may be more important than talk. The parties may be more ready for battle than for cooperatively working out a solution to a common problem. People often come to a negotiation realizing that the stakes are high and feeling threatened. Emotions on one side will generate emotions on the other. Fear may breed anger, and anger, fear. Emotions may quickly bring a negotiation to an impasse or an end.

First recognize and understand emotions, theirs and yours. Look at yourself during the negotiation. Are you feeling nervous? Is your stomach upset? Are you angry at the other side? Listen to them and get a sense of what their emotions are. You may find it useful to write down what you feel — perhaps fearful, worried, angry — and then how you might like to feel — confident, relaxed. Do the same for them.

In dealing with negotiators who represent their organizations, it is easy to treat them as mere mouthpieces without emotions. It is important to remember that they too, like you, have personal feelings, fears, hopes, and dreams. Their careers may be at stake. There may be issues on which they are particularly sensitive and others on which they are particularly proud. Nor are the problems of emotion limited to the negotiators. Constituents have emotions too. A constituent may have an even more simplistic and adversarial view of the situation.

Ask yourself what is producing the emotions. Why are you angry? Why are they angry? Are they responding to past grievances and looking for revenge? Are emotions spilling over from one issue to another? Are personal problems at home interfering with business? In the Middle East negotiation, Israelis and Palestinians alike feel a threat to their existence as peoples and have developed powerful emotions that now permeate even the most concrete practical issue, like distribution of water in the West Bank, so that it becomes almost impossible to discuss and resolve. Because in the larger picture both peoples feel that their own survival is at stake, they see every other issue in terms of survival.

Pay attention to "core concerns." Many emotions in negotiation are driven by a core set of five interests: *autonomy*, the desire to make your own choices and control your own fate; *appreciation*, the desire to be recognized and valued; *affiliation*, the desire to belong as an accepted member of some peer group; *role*, the desire to have a meaningful purpose; and *status*, the desire to feel fairly seen and acknowledged. Trampling on these interests tends to generate strong negative emotions. Attending to them can build rapport and a positive climate for problem-solving negotiation.*

Consider the role of identity. Another surefire driver of strong negative emotion is a perceived threat to identity—one's self-image or self-respect. As human beings, we apply our general tendency toward either-or thinking to our self-perception: "I am a kind person." "I'm a good manager." This sets us up to feel threatened by people pointing out our inevitable failings and inconsistencies. No

---

* For more on the core concerns and how to manage them in negotiation, see Roger Fisher and Daniel Shapiro, *Beyond Reason: Using Emotions As You Negotiate* (Penguin, 2006).

one is perfect or entirely consistent about anything, but unconsciously that can be painful and uncomfortable to accept. As a result, when confronted, we may get scared or angry as an internal debate rages about whether we "are" or "aren't" competent, lovable, fair, or whatever matters to us.

If you find a counterpart's behavior oddly out of character or feel as if you have unexpectedly stepped on a land mine in your conversation, think about whether they might be experiencing a threat to their identity from something you have said or might say. Similarly, if you find yourself feeling off-balance and emotional, ask yourself if your sense of identity feels threatened.*

Make emotions explicit and acknowledge them as legitimate. Talk with the people on the other side about their emotions. Talk about your own. It does not hurt to say, "You know, the people on our side feel we have been mistreated and are very upset. We're afraid an agreement will not be kept even if one is reached. Rational or not, that is our concern. Personally, I think we may be wrong in fearing this, but that's a feeling others have. Do the people on your side feel the same way?" Making your feelings or theirs an explicit focus of discussion will not only underscore the seriousness of the problem, it will also make the negotiations less reactive and more "pro-active." Freed from the burden of unexpressed emotions, people will become more likely to work on the problem.

Allow the other side to let off steam. Often, one effective way to deal with people's anger, frustration, and other negative emotions is to help them release those feelings. People obtain psychological release through the simple process of recounting their grievances to an attentive audience. If you come home wanting to tell your husband about everything that went wrong at the office, you will become even more frustrated if he says, "Don't

---

* For more on identity and other human factors that can get in the way of problem-solving negotiation, see Douglas Stone, Bruce Patton, and Sheila Heen, *Difficult Conversations: How to Discuss What Matters Most* (Viking/Penguin, 1999; 2nd Edition, 2010).

bother telling me; I'm sure you had a hard day. Let's skip it." The same is true for negotiators. Letting off steam may make it easier to talk rationally later. Moreover, if a negotiator makes an angry speech and thereby shows his constituency that he is not being "soft," they may give him a freer hand in the negotiation. He can then rely on a reputation for toughness to protect him from criticism later if he eventually enters into an agreement.

Hence, instead of interrupting polemical speeches or walking out on the other party, you may decide to control yourself, sit there, and allow them to pour out their grievances at you. When constituents are listening, such occasions may release their frustration as well as the negotiator's. Perhaps the best strategy to adopt while the other side lets off steam is to listen quietly without responding to their attacks, and occasionally to ask the speaker to continue until he has spoken his last word. In this way, you offer little support to the inflammatory substance, give the speaker every encouragement to speak himself out, and leave little or no residue to fester.

Don't react to emotional outbursts. Releasing emotions can prove risky if it leads to an emotional reaction. If not controlled, it can result in a violent quarrel. One unusual and effective technique to contain the impact of emotions was used in the 1950s by the Human Relations Committee, a labor-management group set up in the steel industry to handle emerging conflicts before they became serious problems. The members of the committee adopted the rule that only one person could get angry at a time. This made it legitimate for others not to respond stormily to an angry outburst. It also made letting off emotional steam easier by making an outburst itself more legitimate: "That's OK. It's his turn." The rule has the further advantage of helping people control their emotions. Breaking the rule implies that you have lost self-control, so you lose some face.

Use symbolic gestures. Any lover knows that to end a quarrel the simple gesture of bringing a red rose goes a long way. Acts that would produce a constructive emotional impact on one side often involve little or no cost to the other. A note of sympathy, a statement of regret, a visit to a cemetery, delivering a small present for a grandchild, shaking hands or embracing, eating together— all may be priceless opportunities to improve a hostile emotional situation at small cost. On many occasions an apology can defuse emotions effectively, even when you do not acknowledge personal responsibility for the action or admit an intention to harm. An apology may be one of the least costly and most rewarding investments you can make.

Communication

Without communication there is no negotiation. Negotiation is a process of communicating back and forth for the purpose of reaching a joint decision. Communication is never an easy thing, even between people who have an enormous background of shared values and experience. Couples who have lived with each other for thirty years still have misunderstandings every day. It is not surprising, then, to find poor communication between people who do not know each other well and who may feel hostile and suspicious of one another. Whatever you say, you should expect that the other side will almost always hear something different.

There are three big problems in communication. First, negotiators may not be talking to each other, or at least not in such a way as to be understood. Frequently each side has given up on the other and is no longer attempting any serious communication with it. Instead they talk merely to impress third parties or their own constituency. Rather than trying to dance with their negotiating partner toward a mutually agreeable outcome, they try to trip him up. Rather than trying to talk their partner into a more constructive step, they try to talk the spectators into taking sides. Effective communication between the parties is all but impossible if each plays to the gallery.

Even if you are talking directly and clearly to them, they may not be hearing you. This constitutes the second problem in communication. Note how often people don't seem to pay enough attention to what you say. Probably equally often, you would be unable to repeat what they had said. In a negotiation, you may be so busy thinking about what you are going to say next, how you are going to respond to that last point or how you are going to frame your next argument, that you forget to listen to what the other side is saying now. Or you may be listening more attentively to your constituency than to the other side. Your constituents, after all, are the ones to whom you will have to account for the results of the negotiation. They are the ones you are trying to satisfy. It is not surprising that you should want to pay close attention to them. But if you are not hearing what the other side is saying, there is no communication.

The third communication problem is misunderstanding. What one says, the other may misinterpret. Even when negotiators are in the same room, communication from one to the other can seem like sending smoke signals in a high wind. Where the parties speak different languages the chance for misinterpretation is compounded. For example, in Persian, the word "compromise" apparently lacks the positive meaning it has in English of "a midway solution both sides can live with," but has only a negative meaning as in "our integrity was compromised." Similarly, the word "mediator" in Persian suggests "meddler," someone who is barging in uninvited. In early 1980 U.N. Secretary General Kurt Waldheim flew to Iran to seek the release of American diplomats being held hostage by Iranian students soon after the Islamic revolution. His efforts were seriously set back when Iranian national radio and television broadcast in Persian a remark he reportedly made on his arrival in Tehran: "I have come as a *mediator* to work out a *compromise*." Within an hour of the broadcast, his car was being stoned by angry Iranians.

What can be done about these three problems of communication?

Listen actively and acknowledge what is being said. The need for listening is obvious, yet it is difficult to listen well, especially under the stress of an ongoing negotiation. Listening enables you to understand their perceptions, feel their emotions, and hear what they are trying to say. Active listening improves not only what you hear but also what they say. If you pay attention and interrupt occasionally to say, "Did I understand correctly that you are saying that . . . ?" the other side will realize that they are not just killing time, not just going through a routine. They will also feel the satisfaction of being heard and understood. It has been said that the cheapest concession you can make to the other side is to let them know they have been heard.

Standard techniques of good listening are to pay close attention to what is said, to ask the other party to spell out carefully and clearly exactly what they mean, and to request that ideas be repeated if there is any ambiguity or uncertainty. Make it your task while listening not to phrase a response, but to understand them as they see themselves. Take in their perceptions, their needs, and their constraints.

Many consider it a good tactic not to give the other side's case too much attention, and not to admit any legitimacy in their point of view. A good negotiator does just the reverse. Unless you acknowledge what they are saying and demonstrate that you understand them, they may believe you have not heard them. When you then try to explain a different point of view, they will suppose that you still have not grasped what they mean. They will say to themselves, "I told him my view, but now he's saying something different, so he must not have understood it." Then instead of listening to your point, they will be considering how to make their argument in a new way so that this time maybe you will fathom it. So show that you understand them. "Let me see whether I follow what you are telling me. From your point of view, the situation looks like this. . . ."

As you repeat what you understood them to have said, phrase it *positively* from their point of view, making the strength of their case clear. You might say, "You have a strong case. Let me see if I can explain it. Here's the way it strikes me. . . ." Understanding is not agreeing. One can at the same time understand perfectly and disagree completely with what the other side is saying. But unless you can convince them that you do grasp how they see it, you may be unable to get them to hear when you explain your viewpoint to them. Once you have made their case for them, then come back with the problems you find in their proposal. If you can put their case better than they can, and then refute it, you maximize the chance of initiating a constructive dialogue on the merits and minimize the chance of their believing you have misunderstood them.

Speak to be understood. Talk to the other side. It is easy to forget sometimes that a negotiation is not a debate. Nor is it a trial. You are not trying to persuade some third party. The person you are trying to persuade is seated at the table with you. If a negotiation is to be compared with a legal proceeding, the situation resembles that of two judges trying to reach agreement on how to decide a case. Try putting yourself in that role, treating your opposite number as a fellow judge with whom you are attempting to work out a joint opinion. In this context it is clearly unpersuasive to blame the other party for the problem, to engage in name-calling, or to raise your voice. On the contrary, it will help to recognize explicitly that they see the situation differently and to try to go forward as people with a joint problem.

To reduce the dominating and distracting effect that the press, home audiences, and third parties may have, it is useful to establish private and confidential means of communicating with the other side. You can also improve communication by limiting the size of the group meeting. In the negotiations over the city of Trieste in 1954, for example, little progress was made in the talks among Yugoslavia, Britain, and the United States until the three principal negotiators abandoned their large delegations and started meeting alone and informally in a private house. A good case can be made for changing President Woodrow Wilson's appealing slogan "Open covenants openly arrived at" to "Open covenants privately arrived at." No matter how many people are involved in a negotiation, important decisions are typically made when no more than two people are in the room.

Speak about yourself, not about them. In many negotiations, each side explains and condemns at great length the motivations and intentions of the other side. It is more persuasive, however, to describe a problem in terms of its impact on you than in terms of what they did or why: "I feel let down" instead of "You broke your word." "We feel discriminated against" rather than "You're a racist." If you make a statement about them that they believe is untrue, they will ignore you or get angry; they will not focus on your concern. But a statement about how you feel is difficult to challenge. You convey the same information without provoking a defensive reaction that will prevent them from taking it in.

Speak for a purpose. Sometimes the problem is not too little communication, but too much. When anger and misperception are high, some thoughts are best left unsaid. At other times, full disclosure of how flexible you are may make it harder to reach agreement rather than easier. If you let me know that you would be willing to sell your car for $15,000, after I have said that I would be willing to pay as much as $20,000, we may have more trouble striking a deal than if you had just kept quiet. The moral is: Before making a significant statement, know what you want to communicate or find out, and know what purpose this information will serve.

Prevention works best

The techniques just described for dealing with problems of perception, emotion, and communication usually work well. However, the best time for handling people problems is before they become people problems. This means building a personal and organizational relationship with the other side that can cushion the people on each side against the knocks of negotiation. It also means structuring the negotiating game in ways that disentangle the substantive problem from the relationship and protect people's egos from getting involved in substantive discussions.

Build a working relationship. Knowing the other side personally really does help. It is much easier to attribute diabolical intentions to an unknown abstraction called the "other side" than to someone you know personally. Dealing with a classmate, a colleague, a friend, or even a friend of a friend is quite different from dealing with a stranger. The more quickly you can turn a stranger into someone you know, the easier a negotiation is likely to become. You have less difficulty understanding where they are coming from. You have a foundation of trust to build upon in a difficult negotiation. You have smooth, familiar communication routines. It is easier to defuse tension with a joke or an informal aside.

The time to develop such a relationship is before the negotiation begins. Get to know them and find out about their likes and dislikes. Find ways to meet them informally. Try arriving early to chat before the negotiation is scheduled to start, and linger after it ends. Benjamin Franklin's favorite technique was to ask an adversary if he could borrow a certain book. This would flatter the person and give him the comfortable feeling of knowing that Franklin owed him a favor.

Face the problem, not the people. If negotiators view themselves as adversaries in a personal face-to-face confrontation, it is difficult to disentangle their relationship from the substantive problem. In that context, anything one negotiator says about the problem seems to be directed personally at the other and is received that way. Each side tends to become defensive and reactive and to ignore the other side's legitimate interests altogether.

A more effective way for the parties to think of themselves is as partners in a hardheaded, side-by-side search for a fair agreement advantageous to each.

Like two shipwrecked sailors in a lifeboat at sea quarreling over limited rations and supplies, negotiators may begin by seeing each other as adversaries. Each may view the other as a hindrance. To survive, however, those two sailors will want to disentangle the objective problems from the people. They will want to identify the needs of each, whether for shade, medicine, water, or food. They will want to go further and treat the meeting of those needs as a shared problem, along with other shared problems like keeping watch, catching rainwater, and getting the lifeboat to shore. Seeing themselves as engaged in side-by-side efforts to solve a mutual problem, the sailors will become better able to reconcile their conflicting interests as well as to advance their shared interests. Similarly with two negotiators. However difficult personal relations may be between us, you and I become better able to reach an amicable reconciliation of our various interests when we accept that task as a shared problem and face it jointly.

To help the other side change from a face-to-face orientation to side-by-side, you might raise the issue with them explicitly. "Look, we're both lawyers [diplomats, businessmen, family, etc.]. Unless we try to satisfy your interests, we are hardly likely to reach an agreement that satisfies mine, and vice versa. Let's look together at the problem of how to satisfy our collective interests." Alternatively, you could start treating the negotiation as a side-by-side process and by your actions make it desirable for them to join in.

It helps to sit literally on the same side of a table and to have in front of you the contract, the map, the blank pad of paper, or whatever else depicts the problem. If you have established a basis for mutual trust, so much the better. But however precarious your relationship may be, try to structure the negotiation as a side-by-side activity in which the two of you—with your different interests and perceptions, and your emotional involvement—jointly face a common task.

Separating the people from the problem is not something you can do once and forget about; you have to keep working at it. The basic approach is to deal with the people as human beings and with the problem on its merits. How to do the latter is the subject of the next three chapters.

3 Focus on Interests, Not Positions

Consider Mary Parker Follett's story of two men quarreling in a library. One wants the window open and the other wants it closed. They bicker back and forth about how much to leave it open: a crack, halfway, three-quarters of the way. No solution satisfies them both.

Enter the librarian. She asks one why he wants the window open: "To get some fresh air." She asks the other why he wants it closed: "To avoid the draft." After thinking a minute, she opens wide a window in the next room, bringing in fresh air without a draft.

For a wise solution reconcile interests, not positions

This story is typical of many negotiations. Since the parties' problem appears to be a conflict of positions, and since their goal is to agree on a position, they naturally tend to think and talk about positions—and in the process often reach an impasse.

The librarian could not have invented the solution she did if she had focused only on the two men's stated positions of wanting the window open or closed. Instead she looked to their underlying interests of fresh air and no draft. This difference between positions and interests is crucial.

Interests define the problem. The basic problem in a negotiation lies not in conflicting positions, but in the conflict between each side's needs, desires, concerns, and fears. The parties may say:

"I am trying to get him to stop that real estate development next door."

Or "We disagree. He wants $300,000 for the house. I won't pay a penny more than $250,000."

But on a more basic level the problem is:

"He needs the cash; I want peace and quiet."

Or "He needs at least $300,000 to pay off the mortgage and put 20 percent down on his new house. I told my family that I wouldn't pay more than $250,000 for a house."

Such desires and concerns are *interests*. Interests motivate people; they are the silent movers behind the hubbub of positions. Your position is something you have decided upon. Your interests are what caused you to so decide.

The Egyptian-Israeli peace treaty blocked out at the Camp David summit in 1978 demonstrates the usefulness of looking behind positions. Israel had occupied the Egyptian Sinai Peninsula since the Six Day War of 1967. When Egypt and Israel sat down together in 1978 to negotiate a peace, their positions were incompatible. Israel insisted on keeping some of the Sinai. Egypt, on the other hand, insisted that every inch of the Sinai be returned to Egyptian sovereignty. Time and again, people drew maps showing possible boundary lines that would divide the Sinai between Egypt and Israel. Compromising in this way was wholly unacceptable to Egypt. To go back to the situation as it was in 1967 was equally unacceptable to Israel.

Looking to their interests instead of their positions made it possible to develop a solution. Israel's interest lay in security; they did not want Egyptian tanks poised on their border ready to roll across at any time. Egypt's interest lay in sovereignty; the Sinai had been part of Egypt since the time of the Pharaohs. After centuries of domination by Greeks, Romans, Turks, French, and British, Egypt had only recently regained full sovereignty and was not about to cede territory to another foreign conqueror.

At Camp David, President Sadat of Egypt and Prime Minister Begin of Israel agreed to a plan that would return the Sinai to complete Egyptian sovereignty and, by demilitarizing large areas, would still assure Israeli security. The Egyptian flag would fly everywhere, but Egyptian tanks would be nowhere near Israel.

Reconciling interests rather than positions works for two reasons. First, for every interest there usually exist several possible positions that could satisfy it. All too often people simply adopt the most obvious position, as Israel did, for example, in announcing that they intended to keep part of the Sinai. When you do look behind opposed positions for the motivating interests, you can often find an alternative position that meets not only your interests but theirs as well. In the Sinai, demilitarization was one such alternative.

Reconciling interests rather than compromising between positions also works because behind opposed positions lie many more interests than conflicting ones.

Behind opposed positions lie shared and compatible interests, as well as conflicting ones. We tend to assume that because the other side's positions are opposed to ours, their interests must also be opposed. If we have an interest in defending ourselves, then they must want to attack us. If we have an interest in minimizing the rent, then their interest must be to maximize it. In many negotiations, however, a close examination of the underlying interests will reveal the existence of many more interests that are shared or compatible than ones that are opposed.

For example, look at the interests a tenant shares with a prospective landlord:

1. Both want stability. The landlord wants a stable tenant; the tenant wants a permanent address.
2. Both would like to see the apartment well maintained. The tenant is going to live there; the landlord wants to increase the value of the apartment as well as the reputation of the building.
3. Both are interested in a good relationship with each other. The landlord wants a tenant who pays the rent regularly; the tenant wants a responsive landlord who will carry out the necessary repairs.

They may also have interests that do not conflict but simply differ. For example:

1. The tenant may not want to deal with fresh paint, to which he is allergic. The landlord will not want to pay the costs of repainting all the other apartments.
2. The landlord would like the security of a down payment of the first month's rent, and he may want it by tomorrow. The tenant, knowing that this is a good apartment, may be indifferent on the question of paying tomorrow or later.

When weighed against these shared and divergent interests, the opposed interests in minimizing the rent and maximizing the return seem more manageable. The shared interests will likely result in a long lease, an agreement to share the cost of improving the apartment, and efforts by both parties to accommodate each other in the interest of a good relationship. The divergent interests may perhaps be reconciled by a down payment tomorrow and an agreement by the landlord to paint the apartment provided the tenant buys the paint. The precise amount of the rent is all that remains to be settled, and the market for rental apartments may define that fairly well.

Agreement is often made possible precisely because interests differ. You and a shoe-seller may both like money and shoes. Relatively, his interest in the fifty dollars exceeds his interest in a pair of shoes. For you, the situation is reversed: you like the shoes better than the fifty dollars. Hence the deal. Shared interests and differing but complementary interests can both serve as the building blocks for a wise agreement.

How do you identify interests?

The benefit of looking behind positions for interests is clear. How to go about it is less clear. A position is likely to be concrete and explicit; the interests underlying it may well be unexpressed, intangible, and perhaps inconsistent. How do you go about understanding the interests involved in a negotiation, remembering that figuring out *their* interests will be at least as important as figuring out *yours*?

Ask "Why?" One basic technique is to put yourself in their shoes. Examine each position they take, and ask yourself "Why?" Why, for instance, does your landlord prefer to fix the rent—in a five-year lease—year by year? The answer you may come up with, to be protected against increasing costs, is probably one of his interests. You can also ask the landlord himself why he takes a particular position. If you do, make clear that you are asking not for justification of this position, but for an understanding of the needs, hopes, fears, or desires that it serves. "What's your basic concern, Mr. Peters, in wanting the lease to run for no more than three years?"

Ask "Why not?" Think about their choice. One of the most useful ways to uncover interests is first to identify the basic decision that those on the other side probably see you asking them for, and then to ask yourself why they have not made that decision. What interests of theirs stand in the way? If you are trying to change their minds, the starting point is to figure out where their minds are now.

Consider, for example, the negotiations between the United States and Iran in 1980 (shortly after the Islamic Revolution) over the release of the fifty-two U.S. diplomats and embassy personnel taken hostage in Tehran by student militants when the deposed Shah of Iran entered the United States for cancer treatment. The hostage-taking provoked international outrage, and the United States soon imposed sanctions, froze Iranian bank accounts, and allowed private lawsuits to target those assets. Within Iran, however, the students were seen as heroes by some and as politically useful by conservatives, who were seeking to displace more moderate elected officials.

While there were a host of serious obstacles to a resolution of this dispute, the problem is illuminated simply by looking at the choice of a typical student leader. The demand of the United States was clear: "Release the hostages." During much of 1980 each student leader's choice must have looked something like that illustrated by the balance sheet below.

AS OF: Spring 1980

Currently Perceived Choice of: An Iranian student leader
Question Faced: "Shall I press for immediate release of the American hostages?"

If I say yes	**If I say no**
− I sell out the Revolution.	+ I uphold the Revolution.
− I will be criticized as pro-American.	+ I will be praised for defending Islam.
− The others will probably not agree with me (and I may lose power); if they do and we release the hostages, then:	+ We will probably all stick together.
	+ We get fantastic TV coverage to tell the world about our grievances.
− Iran looks weak.	+ Iran looks strong.
− We back down to the U.S.	+ We stand up to the U.S.
− We get nothing (no Shah, no money).	+ We have a chance of getting something (at least our money back).
− We do not know what the U.S. will do.	+ The hostages provide some protection against U.S. intervention.
− I may have to go back to class.	+ I remain an increasingly important political player.
But:	**But:**
+ There is a chance that economic sanctions might end.	− Economic sanctions will no doubt continue.
+ Our relations with other nations, especially in Europe, may improve.	− Our relations with other nations, especially in Europe, will suffer.
	− Inflation and economic problems will continue.
	− There is a risk that the U.S. might take military action (but a martyr's death is the most glorious).

However:

+ The U.S. may make further commitments about our money, nonintervention, ending sanctions, etc.

+ We can always release the hostages later.

If a typical student leader's choice did look even approximately like this, it is understandable why the militant students held the hostages so long: As outrageous and illegal as the original seizure was, once the hostages had been seized it was not irrational for the students to *keep* holding them from one day to the next, waiting for a more promising time to release them.

In constructing the other side's currently perceived choice the first question to ask is "Whose decision do I want to affect?" The second question is what decision people on the other side now see you asking them to make. If *you* have no idea what they think they are being called on to do, *they* may not either. That alone may explain why they are not deciding as you would like.

Now analyze the consequences, as the other side would probably see them, of agreeing or refusing to make the decision you are asking for. You may find a checklist of consequences such as the following helpful in this task:

Impact on my interests

- Will I lose or gain political support?
- Will colleagues criticize or praise me?

Impact on the group's interests

- What will be the short-term consequences? The long-term consequences?
- What will be the economic [political, legal, psychological, military, etc.] consequences?

- What will be the effect on outside supporters and public opinion?
- Will the precedent be good or bad?
- Will making this decision prevent doing something better?
- Is the action consistent with our principles? Is it "right"?
- Can I do it later if I want?

In this entire process it would be a mistake to try for great precision. Only rarely will you deal with a decision-maker who writes down and weighs the pros and cons. You are trying to understand a very human choice, not making a mathematical calculation.

Realize that each side has multiple interests. In almost every negotiation each side will have many interests, not just one. As a tenant negotiating a lease, for example, you may want to obtain a favorable rental agreement, to reach it quickly with little effort, and to maintain a good working relationship with your landlord. You will have not only a strong interest in *affecting* any agreement you reach, but also one in *effecting* an agreement. You will be simultaneously pursuing both your independent and your shared interests.

A common error in diagnosing a negotiating situation is to assume that each person on the other side has the same interests. This is almost never the case. In the 1960s during the Vietnam war, President Lyndon Johnson was in the habit of lumping together all the different members of the government of North Vietnam, the Vietcong resistance in the south, and their various Soviet and Chinese advisers and calling them all collectively "he." "The enemy has to learn that *he* can't cross the United States with impunity. *He* is going to have to learn that aggression doesn't pay." It will be difficult to influence any such "him" (or even "them") to agree to anything if you fail to appreciate the differing interests of the various people and factions involved.

Thinking of negotiation as a two-person, two-sided affair can be illuminating, but it should not blind you to the usual presence of other persons, other sides, and other influences. In one base-

ball salary negotiation the general manager kept insisting that
$500,000 was simply too much for a particular player, although
other teams were paying at least that much to similarly talented
players. In fact the manager felt his position was unjustifiable,
but he had strict instructions from the club's owners to hold firm
without explaining why, because they were in financial difficulties that they did not want the public to hear about.

Whether it is their employer, client, employees, colleagues, family, or spouse, all negotiators have a constituency to whose interests they are sensitive. To understand a negotiator's interests means
to understand the variety of somewhat differing interests that they
need to take into account.

The most powerful interests are basic human needs. In searching for the basic interests behind a declared position, look particularly for those bedrock concerns that motivate all people. If
you can take care of such basic needs, you increase the chance
both of reaching agreement and, if an agreement is reached, of
the other side's keeping to it. Basic human needs include:

- security
- economic well-being
- a sense of belonging
- recognition
- control over one's life

As fundamental as they are, basic human needs are easy to
overlook. In many negotiations, we tend to think that the only
interest involved is money. Yet even in a negotiation over a mon-
etary figure, such as the amount of alimony to be specified in a
separation agreement, much more can be involved. What does a
spouse really want in asking for $1,000 a week in alimony? Cer-
tainly they are interested in economic well-being, but what else?
Possibly they want the money in order to feel psychologically
secure. They may also want it for recognition: to feel treated
fairly and as an equal. Perhaps their partner can ill afford to pay

$1,000 a week, and perhaps that is more than is actually needed, yet the spouse will likely accept less only if their need for security and recognition are met in other ways.

What is true for individuals remains equally true for groups and nations. Negotiations are not likely to make much progress as long as one side believes that the fulfillment of their basic human needs is being threatened by the other. In negotiations between the United States and Mexico, the United States wanted a low price for Mexican natural gas. Assuming that this was a negotiation over money, the U.S. Secretary of Energy refused to approve a price increase negotiated with the Mexicans by a U.S. oil consortium. Since the Mexicans had no other potential buyer at the time, he assumed that they would then lower their asking price. But the Mexicans had a strong interest not only in getting a good price for their gas but also in being treated with respect and a sense of equality. The U.S. action seemed like one more attempt to bully Mexico; it produced enormous anger. Rather than sell their gas, the Mexican government began to burn it off, and any chance of agreement on a lower price became politically impossible.

To take another example, in negotiations over the future of Northern Ireland, Protestant leaders long tended to ignore the Catholics' need for both belonging and recognition, for being accepted and treated as equals. In turn, Catholic leaders often appeared to give too little weight to the Protestants' need to feel secure. Treating Protestant fears as "their problem" rather than as a legitimate concern needing attention made it even more difficult to negotiate a solution.

Make a list. To sort out the various interests of each side, it helps to write them down as they occur to you. This will not only help you remember them; it will also enable you to improve the quality of your assessment as you learn new information and to place interests in their estimated order of importance. Furthermore, it may stimulate ideas for how to meet these interests.

Talking about interests

The purpose of negotiating is to serve your interests. The chance of that happening increases when you communicate them. The other side may not know what your interests are, and you may not know theirs. One or both of you may be focusing on past grievances instead of on future concerns. Or you may not even be listening to each other. How do you discuss interests constructively without getting locked into rigid positions?

If you want the other side to take your interests into account, explain to them what those interests are. A member of a concerned citizens' group complaining about a construction project in the neighborhood should talk explicitly about such issues as ensuring children's safety and getting a good night's sleep. An author who wants to be able to give a great many of his books away should discuss the matter with his publisher. The publisher has a shared interest in promotion and may be willing to offer the author a low price.

Make your interests come alive. If you go with a raging ulcer to see a doctor, you should not hope for much relief if you describe it as a mild stomachache. It is your job to have the other side understand exactly how important and legitimate your interests are.

One guideline is *be specific.* Concrete details not only make your description credible, they add impact. For example: "Three times in the last week, a child was almost run over by one of your trucks. About eight-thirty Tuesday morning that huge red gravel truck of yours, going north at almost forty miles an hour, had to swerve and barely missed hitting seven-year-old Loretta Johnson."

As long as you do not seem to imply that the other side's interests are unimportant or illegitimate, you can afford to take a strong stance in setting forth the seriousness of your concerns. Inviting the other side to "correct me if I'm wrong" shows your openness, and if they do not correct you, it implies that they accept your description of the situation.

Part of the task of impressing the other side with your interests lies in establishing the legitimacy of those interests. You want them to feel not that you are attacking them personally, but rather that the problem you face legitimately demands attention. You need to convince them that they might well feel the same way if they were in your shoes. "Do you have children? How would you feel if trucks were hurtling at forty miles per hour down the street where you live?"

Acknowledge their interests as part of the problem. Each of us tends to be so concerned with his or her own interests that we pay too little heed to the interests of others.

People listen better if they feel that you have understood them. They tend to think that those who understand them are intelligent and sympathetic people whose own opinions may be worth listening to. So if you want the other side to appreciate *your* interests, begin by demonstrating that you appreciate *theirs*.

"As I understand it, your interests as a construction company are basically to get the job done quickly at minimum cost and to preserve your reputation for safety and responsibility in the city. Have I understood you correctly? Do you have other important interests?"

In addition to demonstrating that you have understood their interests, it helps to acknowledge that their interests are part of the overall problem you are trying to solve. This is especially easy to do if you have shared interests: "It would be terrible for all of us if one of your trucks hit a child."

Put the problem before your answer. In talking to someone who represents a construction company, you might say, "We believe you should build a fence around the project within forty-eight hours and beginning immediately should restrict the speed of your trucks on Oak Street to fifteen miles per hour. Now let me tell you why. . . ." If you do, you can be quite certain that the representatives will not be listening to the reasons. They have heard your position and are no doubt busy preparing arguments against it. They probably were disturbed by your tone or by the suggestion itself. As a result, your justification will slip by them altogether.

If you want someone to listen and understand your reasoning, give your interests and reasoning first and your conclusions or proposals later. Tell the company first about the dangers they are creating for young children and about your sleepless nights. Then they will be listening carefully, if only to try to figure out where you will end up on this question. And when you tell them, they will understand why.

Look forward, not back. It is surprising how often we simply react to what someone else has said or done. Two people will often fall into a pattern of discourse that resembles a negotiation, but really has no such purpose whatsoever. They disagree with each other over some issue, and the talk goes back and forth as though they were seeking agreement. In fact, the argument is being carried on as a ritual, or simply a pastime. Each is engaged in scoring points against the other or in gathering evidence to confirm views about the other that have long been held and are not about to change. Neither party is seeking agreement or is even trying to influence the other.

If you ask two people why they are arguing, the answer will typically identify a cause, not a purpose. Caught up in a quarrel, whether between husband and wife, between company and union, or between two businesses, people are more likely to respond to what the other side has said or done than to act in pursuit of their own long-term interests. "They can't treat me like that. If they think they're going to get away with that, they will have to think again. I'll show them."

The question "Why?" has two quite different meanings. One looks backward for a cause and treats our behavior as determined by prior events. The other looks forward for a purpose and treats our behavior as subject to our free will. We need not enter into a philosophical debate between free will and determinism in order to decide how to act. Either we have free will or it is determined that we behave as if we do. In either case, we make choices. We can *choose* to look back or to look forward.

You will satisfy your interests better if you talk about where you would like to go rather than about where you have come from. Instead of arguing with the other side about the past—about last quarter's costs (which were too high), last week's action (taken without adequate authority), or yesterday's performance (which was less than expected)—talk about what you want to have happen in the future. Instead of asking them to justify what they did yesterday, ask, "Who should do what tomorrow?"

Be concrete but flexible. In a negotiation you want to know where you are going and yet be open to fresh ideas. To avoid having to make a difficult decision on what to settle for, people will often go into a negotiation with no plan other than to sit down with the other side and see what they offer or demand.

How can you move from identifying interests to developing specific options and still remain flexible with regard to those options? To convert your interests into concrete options, ask yourself, "If tomorrow the other side agrees to go along with me, what do I now think I would like them to go along with?" To keep your flexibility, treat each option you formulate as simply illustrative. Think in terms of more than one option that meets your interests. "Illustrative specificity" is the key concept.

Much of what positional bargainers hope to achieve with an opening position can be accomplished equally well with an illustrative suggestion that generously takes care of your interest. For example, in a sports contract negotiation, an agent might say that "$5,000,000 a year would be the kind of figure that should satisfy Henderson's interest in receiving the salary he feels he is worth. Something on the order of a five-year contract should meet his need for job security."

Having thought about your interests, you should go into a meeting not only with one or more specific options that would meet your legitimate interests but also with an open mind. An open mind is not an empty one.

Be hard on the problem, soft on the people. You can be just as hard in talking about your interests as any negotiator can be in talking about their position. In fact, it is usually advisable to be hard. It may not be wise to commit yourself to your position, but it is wise to commit yourself to your interests. This is the place in a negotiation to spend your aggressive energies. The other side, being concerned with their own interests, will tend to have overly optimistic expectations of the range of possible agreements. Often the wisest solutions, those that produce the maximum gain for you at the minimum cost to the other side, are produced only by strongly advocating your interests. Two negotiators, each pushing hard for their interests, will often stimulate each other's creativity in thinking up mutually advantageous solutions.

The construction company, concerned with inflation, may place a high value on its interest in keeping costs down and in getting the job done on time. You may have to shake them up. Some honest emotion may help restore a better balance between profits and children's lives. Do not let your desire to be conciliatory stop you from doing justice to your problem. "Surely you're not saying that my son's life is worth less than the price of a fence. You wouldn't say that about your son. I don't believe you're an insensitive person, Mr. Jenkins. Let's figure out how to solve this problem."

If they feel personally threatened by an attack on the problem, they may grow defensive and may cease to listen. This is why it is important to separate the people from the problem. Attack the problem without blaming the people. Go even further and be personally supportive: Listen to them with respect, show them courtesy, express your appreciation for their time and effort, emphasize your concern with meeting their basic needs, and so on. Show them that you are attacking the *problem*, not them.

One useful rule of thumb is to give positive support to the human beings on the other side equal in strength to the vigor with which you emphasize the problem. This combination of support and attack may seem inconsistent. Psychologically, it is; the inconsistency helps make it work. A well-known theory of psychology, the theory of cognitive dissonance, holds that people dislike inconsistency and will act to eliminate it. By attacking a problem, such as speeding trucks on a neighborhood street, and at the same time giving the company representative, Mr. Jenkins, positive support, you create cognitive dissonance for him. To overcome this dissonance, he will be tempted to dissociate himself from the problem in order to join you in doing something about it.

Fighting hard on the substantive issues increases the pressure for an effective solution; giving support to the human beings on the other side tends to improve your relationship and to increase the likelihood of reaching agreement. It is the combination of support and attack that works; either alone is likely to be insufficient.

Negotiating hard for your interests does not mean being closed to the other side's point of view. Quite the contrary. You can hardly expect the other side to listen to your interests and discuss the options you suggest if you don't take their interests into account and show yourself to be open to their suggestions. Successful negotiation requires being both firm *and* open.

4   Invent Options for
Mutual Gain

The case of Israel and Egypt negotiating over who should keep how much of the Sinai Peninsula illustrates both a major problem in negotiation and a key opportunity.

The problem is a common one. There seems to be no way to split the pie that leaves both parties satisfied. Often you are negotiating along a single dimension, such as the amount of territory, the price of a car, the length of a lease on an apartment, or the size of a commission on a sale. At other times you face what appears to be an either/or choice that is either markedly favorable to you or to the other side. In a divorce settlement, who gets the house? Who gets custody of the children? You may see the choice as one between winning and losing—and neither side will agree to lose. Even if you do win and get the car for $15,000, the lease for five years, or the house and kids, you have a sinking feeling that they will not let you forget it. Whatever the situation, your choices seem limited.

The Sinai example also makes clear the opportunity. A creative option like a demilitarized Sinai can often make the difference between deadlock and agreement. One lawyer we know attributes his success directly to his ability to invent solutions advantageous to both his client and the other side. He expands the pie before dividing it. Skill at inventing options is one of the most useful assets a negotiator can have.

Yet all too often negotiators end up like the proverbial children who quarreled over an orange. After they finally agreed to divide the orange in half, the first child took one half, ate the fruit, and threw away the peel, while the other threw away the fruit and used the peel from the second half in baking a cake. All too often negotiators "leave money on the table"—they fail to reach agreement when they might have, or the agreement they do reach could have been better for each side. Too many negotiations end up with half an orange for each side instead of the whole fruit for one and the whole peel for the other. Why?

DIAGNOSIS

As valuable as it is to have many options, people involved in a negotiation rarely sense a need for them. In a dispute, people usually believe that they know the right answer—their view should prevail. In a contract negotiation they are equally likely to believe that their offer is reasonable and should be adopted, perhaps with some adjustment in the price. All available answers appear to lie along a straight line between their position and yours. Often the only creative thinking shown is to suggest splitting the difference.

In most negotiations there are four major obstacles that inhibit the inventing of an abundance of options: (1) premature judgment; (2) searching for the single answer; (3) the assumption of a fixed pie; and (4) thinking that "solving their problem is their problem." To overcome these constraints, you need to understand them.

Premature judgment

Inventing options does not come naturally. *Not* inventing is the normal state of affairs, even when you are outside a stressful negotiation. If you were asked to name the one person in the world most deserving of the Nobel Peace Prize, any answer you might start to propose would immediately encounter your reservations and doubts. How could you be sure that that person was the *most* deserving? Your mind might well go blank, or you might throw out a few answers that would reflect conventional thinking: "Well, maybe the Pope, or the President."

Nothing is so harmful to inventing as a critical sense waiting to pounce on the drawbacks of any new idea. Judgment hinders imagination.

Under the pressure of a forthcoming negotiation, your critical sense is likely to be sharper. Practical negotiation appears to call for practical thinking, not wild ideas.

Your creativity may be even more stifled by the presence of those on the other side. Suppose you are negotiating with your boss over your salary for the coming year. You have asked for a $4,000 raise; your boss has offered you $1,500, a figure that you have indicated is unsatisfactory. In a tense situation like this you are not likely to start inventing imaginative solutions. You may fear that if you suggest some bright half-baked idea like taking half the increase in a raise and half in additional benefits, you might look foolish. Your boss might say, "Be serious. You know better than that. It would upset company policy. I am surprised that you even suggested it." If on the spur of the moment you invent a possible option of spreading out the raise over time, your boss may take it as an offer: "I'm prepared to start negotiating on that basis." Since whatever you say may be taken as a commitment, you will think twice before saying anything.

You may also fear that by inventing options you will disclose some piece of information that will jeopardize your bargaining position. If you should suggest, for example, that the company help finance the house you are about to buy, your boss may conclude that you intend to stay and that you will in the end accept any raise in salary the boss decides to offer.

Searching for the single answer

In most people's minds, inventing simply is not part of the negotiating process. People see their job as narrowing the gap between positions, not broadening the options available. They tend to think, "We're having a hard enough time agreeing as it is. The last thing we need is a bunch of different ideas." Since the end product of negotiation is a single decision, they fear that free-floating discussion will only delay and confuse the process.

If the first impediment to creative thinking is premature criticism, the second is premature closure. By looking from the outset for the single best answer, you are likely to short-circuit a wiser decision-making process in which you select from a large number of possible answers.

The assumption of a fixed pie

A third explanation for why there may be so few good options on the table is that each side sees the situation as essentially either/or—either I get what is in dispute or you do. A negotiation often appears to be a "fixed-sum" game; $100 more for you on the price of a car means $100 less for me. Why bother to invent if all the options are obvious and I can satisfy you only at my own expense?

Thinking that "solving their problem is their problem"

A final obstacle to inventing realistic options lies in each side's concern with only its own immediate interests. For you as a negotiator to reach an agreement that meets your own self-interest, you need to develop a solution that also appeals to the self-interest of the other. Yet emotional involvement on one side of an issue makes it difficult to achieve the detachment necessary to think up wise ways of meeting the interests of both sides: "We've got enough problems of our own; they can look after theirs." There also frequently exists a psychological reluctance to accord any legitimacy to the views of the other side; it seems disloyal to think up ways to satisfy them. Shortsighted self-concern thus leads a negotiator to develop only partisan positions, partisan arguments, and one-sided solutions.

PRESCRIPTION

To invent creative options, then, you will need to (1) separate the act of inventing options from the act of judging them; (2) broaden the options on the table rather than look for a single answer; (3) search for mutual gains; and (4) invent ways of making their decisions easy. Each of these steps is discussed below.

Separate inventing from deciding

Since judgment hinders imagination, separate the creative act from the critical one; separate the process of thinking up possible decisions from the process of selecting among them. Invent first, decide later.

As a negotiator, you will of necessity do much inventing by yourself. It is not easy. By definition, inventing new ideas requires you to think about things that are not already in your mind. You should therefore consider the desirability of arranging an inventing or brainstorming session with a few colleagues or friends. Such a session can effectively separate inventing from deciding.

A brainstorming session is designed to produce as many ideas as possible to solve the problem at hand. The key ground rule is to postpone all criticism and evaluation of ideas. The group simply invents ideas without pausing to consider whether they are good or bad, realistic or unrealistic. With those inhibitions removed, one idea should stimulate another, like firecrackers setting off one another.

In a brainstorming session, people need not fear looking foolish since wild ideas are explicitly encouraged. And in the absence of the other side, negotiators need not worry about disclosing confidential information or having a half-baked idea taken as a serious commitment.

There is no right way to run a brainstorming session. Rather, you should tailor it to your needs and resources. In doing so, you may find it useful to consider the following guidelines.

Before brainstorming:

1. *Define your purpose.* Think of what you would like to walk out of the meeting with.

2. *Choose a few participants.* The group should normally be large enough to provide a stimulating interchange, yet small enough to encourage both individual participation and free-wheeling inventing—usually between five and eight people.

3. *Change the environment.* Select a time and place distinguishing the session as much as possible from regular discussions. The more different a brainstorming session seems from a normal meeting, the easier it is for participants to suspend judgment.

4. *Design an informal atmosphere.* What does it take for you and others to relax? It may be talking over a drink, or meeting at a vacation lodge in some picturesque spot, or dressing less formally during the meeting and calling one another by your first names.

5. *Choose a facilitator.* Someone at the meeting needs to facilitate—to keep the meeting on track, to make sure everyone gets a chance to speak, to enforce any ground rules, and to stimulate discussion by asking questions.

During brainstorming:

1. *Seat the participants side by side facing the problem.* The physical reinforces the psychological. Physically sitting side by side can reinforce the mental attitude of tackling a common problem together. People facing each other tend to respond personally and engage in dialogue or argument; people sitting side by side in a semicircle of chairs facing a flip chart or whiteboard tend to respond to the problem depicted there.

2. *Clarify the ground rules, including the no-criticism rule.* If the participants do not all know each other, the meeting begins with introductions all around, followed by clarification of the ground rules. Outlaw negative criticism of any kind.

Joint inventing produces new ideas because each of us invents only within the limits set by our working assumptions. If ideas are shot down unless they appeal to all participants, the implicit goal becomes to advance an idea that no one will shoot down. If, on the other hand, wild ideas are encouraged, even those that in fact lie well outside the realm of the possible, the group may generate from these ideas other options that *are* possible and that no one would previously have considered.

Other ground rules you may want to adopt are to make the entire session off the record and to refrain from attributing ideas to any participant.

3. *Brainstorm.* Once the purpose of the meeting is clear, let your imaginations go. Try to come up with a long list of ideas, approaching the question from every conceivable angle.

4. *Record the ideas in full view.* Recording ideas either on a whiteboard or flipcharts gives the group a tangible sense of collective achievement; it reinforces the no-criticism rule; it reduces the tendency to repeat; and it helps stimulate other ideas.

After brainstorming:

1. *Star the most promising ideas.* After brainstorming, relax the no-criticism rule to begin winnowing out the most promising ideas. You are still not at the stage of deciding; you are merely nominating ideas worth developing further. Mark those ideas that members of the group think are best.

2. *Invent improvements for promising ideas.* Take one promising idea and invent ways to make it better and more realistic, as well as ways to carry it out. The task at this stage is to make the idea as attractive as you can. Preface constructive criticism with: "What I like best about that idea is . . . . Might it be even better if . . . ?"

3. *Set up a time to evaluate ideas and decide.* Before you break, draw up a selective and improved list of ideas from the session and set up a time for deciding which of these ideas to advance in your negotiation and how.

Consider brainstorming with the other side. Although more difficult than brainstorming with your own side, brainstorming with people from the other side can also prove extremely valuable. It is more difficult because of the increased risk that you will say something that prejudices your interests despite the rules established for a brainstorming session. You may disclose confidential information inadvertently or lead the other side to mistake an option you devise for an offer. Nevertheless, joint brainstorming sessions have the great advantages of producing ideas that take into account the interests of all those involved, of creating a climate of joint problem-solving, and of educating each side about the concerns of the other.

To protect yourself when brainstorming with the other side, distinguish the brainstorming session explicitly from a negotiating session where people state official views and speak on the record. People are so accustomed to meeting for the purpose of reaching agreement that any other purpose needs to be clearly stated.

To reduce the risk of appearing committed to any given idea, you can make a habit of advancing at least two alternatives at the same time. You can also put on the table options with which you obviously disagree. "I could give you the house for nothing, or you could pay me a million dollars in cash for it, or . . . ." Since you are plainly not proposing either of these ideas, the ones that follow are labeled as mere possibilities, not proposals.

To get the flavor of a joint brainstorming session, let us suppose the leaders of a local union are meeting with the management of a coal mine to brainstorm on ways to reduce unauthorized one- or two-day strikes. Ten people—five from each side—are present, sitting around a table facing a whiteboard. A neutral facilitator asks the participants for their ideas, and writes them up on the whiteboard.

Facilitator: OK, now let's see what ideas you have for dealing with this problem of unauthorized work stoppages. Let's try to get ten ideas on the whiteboard in five minutes. OK, let's start. Tom?

Tom (Union): Foremen ought to be able to settle a union member's grievance on the spot.

Facilitator: Good, I've got it down. Jim, you've got your hand up.

Jim (Management): A union member ought to talk to his foreman about a problem before taking any action that—

Tom (Union): They do, but the foremen don't listen.

Facilitator: Tom, please, no criticizing yet. We agreed to postpone that until later, OK? How about you, Jerry? You look like you've got an idea.

Jerry (Union): When a strike issue comes up, the union members should be allowed to meet in the bathhouse immediately.

Roger (Management): Management could agree to let the bathhouse be used for union meetings and could assure the employees' privacy by shutting the doors and keeping the foremen out.

Carol (Management): How about adopting the rule that there will be no strike without giving the union leaders and management a chance to work it out on the spot?

Jerry (Union): How about speeding up the grievance procedure and having a meeting within twenty-four hours if the foreman and union member don't settle it between themselves?

Karen (Union): Yeah. And how about organizing some joint training for the union members and the foremen on how to handle their problems together?

Phil (Union): If a person does a good job, let him know it.

John (Management): Establish friendly relations between union people and management people.

Facilitator: That sounds promising, John, but could you be more specific?

John (Management): Well, how about organizing a union–management softball team?

Tom (Union): And a bowling team too.

Roger (Management): How about an annual picnic get-together for all the families?

And on it goes, as the participants brainstorm lots of ideas. Many of the ideas might never have come up except in such a brainstorming session, and some of them may prove effective in reducing unauthorized strikes. Time spent brainstorming together is surely among the best-spent time in negotiation.

But whether you brainstorm together or not, separating the act of developing options from the act of deciding on them is extremely useful in any negotiation. Discussing options differs radically from taking positions. Whereas one side's position will conflict with another's, options invite other options. The very language you use differs. It consists of questions, not assertions; it is open, not closed: "One option is . . . . What other options have you thought of?" "What if we agreed to this?" "How about doing it this way?" "How would this work?" "What would be wrong with that?" Invent before you decide.

Broaden your options

Even with the best of intentions, participants in a brainstorming session are likely to operate on the assumption that they are really looking for the *one* best answer, trying to find a needle in a haystack by picking up every blade of hay.

At this stage in a negotiation, however, you should not be looking for the right path. You are developing room within which to negotiate. Room can be made only by having a substantial number of markedly different ideas—ideas on which you and the other side can build later in the negotiation, and among which you can then jointly choose.

A vintner making a fine wine chooses his grapes from a number of varieties. A sports team looking for star players will send talent scouts to scour the local leagues and college teams all over the nation. The same principle applies to negotiation. The key to wise decision-making, whether in wine-making, sports, or negotiation, lies in selecting from a great number and variety of options.

If you were asked who should receive the Nobel Peace Prize this year, you would do well to answer "Well, let's think about it" and generate a list of about a hundred names from diplomacy, business, journalism, religion, law, agriculture, politics, academia,

medicine, and other fields, making sure to dream up a lot of wild
ideas. You would almost certainly end up with a better decision
this way than if you tried to decide right from the start.

A brainstorming session frees people to think creatively. Once
freed, they need ways to think about their problems and to generate constructive solutions.

**Multiply options by shuttling between the specific and the gen-
eral: The Circle Chart.** The task of inventing options involves four
types of thinking. One is thinking about a particular problem—the
factual situation you dislike, for example, a smelly, polluted river
that runs by your land. The second type of thinking is descriptive
analysis—you diagnose an existing situation in general terms. You
sort problems into categories and tentatively suggest causes. The
river water may have a high content of various chemicals, or too
little oxygen. You may suspect various upstream industrial plants.
The third type of thinking, again in general terms, is to consider
what ought, perhaps, to be done. Given the diagnoses you have
made, you look for prescriptions that theory may suggest, such as
reducing chemical effluent, reducing diversions of water, or bringing fresh water from some other river. The fourth and final type of
thinking is to come up with some specific and feasible suggestions
for action. Who might do what tomorrow to put one of these
general approaches into practice? For instance, the state environmental agency might order an upstream industry to limit the quantity of chemical discharge.

The Circle Chart on the next page illustrates these four types
of thinking and suggests them as steps to be taken in sequence. If
all goes well, the specific action invented in this way will, if adopted, deal with your original problem.

The Circle Chart provides an easy way of using one good idea
to generate others. With one useful action idea before you, you
(or a group of you who are brainstorming) can go back and try
to identify the general approach of which the action idea is
merely one application. You can then think up other action ideas
that would apply the same general approach to the real world.
Similarly, you can go back one step further and ask, "If this theo-

CIRCLE CHART
The Four Basic Steps in Inventing Options

WHAT IS WRONG   **WHAT MIGHT BE DONE**

IN THEORY

Step II. Analysis
Diagnose the problem:
Sort symptoms into
   categories.
Suggest causes.
Observe what is lacking.
Note barriers to resolv-
   ing the problem.

Step III. Approaches
What are possible strat-
   egies or prescriptions?
What are some theo-
   retical cures?
Generate broad ideas
   about what might be
   done.

Step I. Problem
What's wrong?
What are current
   symptoms?
What are disliked
   facts contrasted
   with a preferred
   situation?

Step IV. Action Ideas
What might be done?
What specific steps
   might be taken
   to deal with the
   problem?

IN THE REAL WORLD

retical approach appears useful, what is the diagnosis behind it?" Having articulated a diagnosis, you can generate other approaches for dealing with a problem analyzed in that way, and then look for actions putting these new approaches into practice.

One good option on the table thus opens the door to asking about the theory that makes this option good and then using that theory to invent more options.

An example may illustrate the process. In thinking about how to deal with the conflict in Northern Ireland, one idea generated in the 1980s was to have Catholic and Protestant teachers prepare a common workbook on the history of Northern Ireland for use in the primary grades of both school systems. The book, which was actually created and used in the 1990s, presents Northern Irish history as seen from different points of view and gives the children exercises that involve role-playing and putting themselves in other people's shoes. More useful ideas were then generated by starting with this specific action suggestion and asking what theoretical approaches underlay it. This resulted in such general propositions as:

"There should be some common educational content in the two school systems."

"Catholics and Protestants should work together on small, manageable projects."

"Understanding should be promoted in young children before it is too late."

"History should be taught in ways that illuminate partisan perceptions."

Working from these theories additional action suggestions were invented, including a joint Catholic and Protestant film project that presents the history of Northern Ireland as seen through different eyes, a teacher exchange program, and having some common classes for primary-age children in the two systems.

Look through the eyes of different experts. Another way to generate multiple options is to examine your problem from the perspective of different professions and disciplines.

In thinking up possible solutions to a dispute over custody of a child, for example, look at the problem as it might be seen by an educator, a banker, a psychiatrist, a civil rights lawyer, a minister, a nutritionist, a doctor, a feminist, a football coach, or one with some other special point of view. If you are negotiating a business contract, invent options that might occur to a banker, an inventor, a labor leader, a speculator in real estate, a stockbroker, an economist, a tax expert, or a socialist.

You can also combine the use of the Circle Chart with this idea of looking at a problem through the eyes of different experts. Consider in turn how each expert would diagnose the situation, what kinds of approaches each might suggest, and what practical suggestions would follow from those approaches.

Invent agreements of different strengths. You can multiply the number of possible agreements on the table by thinking of "weaker" versions you might want to have on hand in case a sought-for agreement proves beyond reach. If you cannot agree on substance, perhaps you can agree on procedure. If a shoe factory cannot agree with a wholesaler on who should pay for a shipment of damaged shoes, perhaps they can agree to submit the issue to an arbitrator. Similarly, where a permanent agreement is not possible, perhaps a provisional agreement is. At the very least, if you and the other side cannot reach first-order agreement, you can usually reach second-order agreement—that is, agree on where you disagree, so that you both know the issues in dispute, which are not always obvious. The pairs of adjectives below suggest potential agreements of differing "strengths":

Stronger	Weaker
Substantive	Procedural
Permanent	Provisional
Comprehensive	Partial
Final	In principle
Unconditional	Contingent
Binding	Nonbinding
First-order	Second-order

Change the scope of a proposed agreement. Consider the possibility of varying not only the strength of the agreement but also its scope. You could, for instance, "fractionate" your problem into smaller and perhaps more manageable units. To a prospective editor for your book, you might suggest: "How about editing the first chapter for $300, and we'll see how it goes?" Agreements may be partial, involve fewer parties, cover only selected subject matters, apply only to a certain geographical area, or remain in effect for only a limited period of time.

It is also provocative to ask how the subject matter might be enlarged so as to "sweeten the pot" and make agreement more attractive. The dispute between India and Pakistan over the waters of the Indus River became more amenable to settlement when the World Bank entered the discussions; the parties were challenged to invent new irrigation projects, new storage dams, and other engineering works for the benefit of both nations, all to be funded with the assistance of the Bank.

Look for mutual gain

The third major block to creative problem-solving lies in the assumption of a fixed pie: the less for you, the more for me. Rarely if ever is this assumption true. First of all, both sides can always be worse off than they are now. Chess looks like a zero-sum game; if one loses, the other wins — until a dog trots by and knocks over the table, spills the beer, and leaves you both worse off than before.

Even apart from a shared interest in averting joint loss, there almost always exists the possibility of joint gain. This may take the form of developing a mutually advantageous relationship, or of satisfying the interests of each side with a creative solution.

Identify shared interests. In theory it is obvious that shared interests help produce agreement. By definition, inventing an idea that meets shared interests is good for you and good for them. In practice, however, the picture seems less clear. In the middle of a negotiation over price, shared interests may not appear obvious or relevant. How then can looking for shared interests help?

Let's take an example. Suppose you are the manager of an oil refinery. Call it Townsend Oil. The mayor of Pageville, the city where the refinery is located, has told you he wants to raise the taxes Townsend Oil pays to Pageville from two million dollars a year to four million. You have told him that you think two million a year is quite sufficient. The negotiation stands there: he wants more, you want to pay what you have been paying. In this negotiation, a typical one in many ways, where do shared interests come into play?

Let's take a closer look at what the mayor wants. He wants money—money undoubtedly to pay for city services, a new civic center, perhaps, and to relieve the ordinary taxpayers. But the city cannot obtain all the money it needs for now and for the future just from Townsend Oil. They will look for money from the petrochemical plant across the street, for example, and, for the future, from new businesses and from the expansion of existing businesses. The mayor, a businessman himself, would also like to encourage industrial expansion and attract new businesses that will provide new jobs and strengthen Pageville's economy.

What are your company's interests? Given the rapid changes in the technology of refining oil, and the antiquated condition of your refinery, you are presently considering a major refurbishment and expansion of the plant. You are concerned that the city may later increase its assessment of the value of the expanded refinery, thus making taxes even higher. Consider also that you have been encouraging a plastics plant to locate itself nearby to make convenient use of your product. Naturally, you worry that the plastics plant will have second thoughts once they see the city increasing taxes.

The shared interests between the mayor and you now become more apparent. You both agree on the goals of fostering industrial expansion and encouraging new industries. If you did some inventing to meet these shared goals, you might come up with several ideas: a tax holiday of seven years for new industries, a joint publicity campaign with the Chamber of Commerce to attract new companies, a reduction in taxes for existing industries that choose to expand. Such ideas might save you money while still filling the city's coffers. If on the other hand the negotiation soured the relationship between company and town, both would lose. You might cut back on your corporate contributions to city charities and school athletics. The city might become unreasonably tough in enforcing the building code and other ordinances. Your personal relationship with the city's political and business leaders might grow unpleasant. The relationship between the sides, often taken for granted and overlooked, frequently outweighs in importance the outcome of any particular issue.

As a negotiator, you will almost always want to look for solutions that will leave the other side satisfied as well. If the customer feels cheated in a purchase, the store owner has also failed; he may lose a customer and his reputation may suffer. An outcome in which the other side gets absolutely nothing is worse for you than one that leaves them mollified. In almost every case, your satisfaction depends to a degree on making the other side sufficiently content with an agreement to want to live up to it.

Three points about shared interests are worth remembering. First, shared interests lie latent in every negotiation. They may not be immediately obvious. Ask yourself: Do we have a shared interest in preserving our relationship? What opportunities lie ahead for cooperation and mutual benefit? What costs would we bear if negotiations broke off? Are there common principles, like a fair price, that we both can respect?

Second, shared interests are opportunities, not godsends. To be of use, you need to make something out of them. It helps to make a shared interest explicit and to formulate it as a shared *goal*. In other words, make it concrete and future-oriented. As manager of Townsend Oil, for example, you could set a joint goal with the mayor of bringing five new industries into Pageville within three years. The tax holiday for new industries would then represent not a concession by the mayor to you but an action in pursuit of your shared goal.

Third, stressing your shared interests can make the negotiation smoother and more amicable. Passengers in a lifeboat afloat in the middle of the ocean with limited rations will subordinate their differences over food in pursuit of their shared interest in getting to shore.

Dovetail differing interests. Consider once again the two children quarreling over an orange. Each child wanted the orange, so they split it, failing to realize that one wanted only the fruit to eat and the other only the peel for baking. In this case as in many others, a satisfactory agreement is made possible because each side wants *different* things. This is genuinely startling if you think about it. People generally assume that differences between two parties create the problem. Yet differences can also lead to a solution.

Agreement is often based on disagreement. It is as absurd to think, for example, that you should always begin by reaching agreement on the facts as it is for a buyer of stock to try to convince the seller that the stock is likely to go up. If they did agree that the stock would go up, the seller would probably not sell. What makes a deal likely is that the buyer believes the price will go up and the seller believes it will go down. The difference in belief provides the basis for a deal.

Many creative agreements reflect this principle of reaching agreement through differences. Differences in interests and belief make it possible for an item to be of high benefit to you, yet low cost to the other side. Consider the nursery rhyme:

> Jack Sprat could eat no fat
> His wife could eat no lean,
> And so betwixt them both
> They licked the platter clean.

The kinds of differences that best lend themselves to dovetailing are differences in interests, in beliefs, in the value placed on time, in forecasts, and in aversion to risk.

Any difference in interests? The following brief checklist suggests common variations in interest to look for:

One party cares more about:	The other party cares more about:
Form	Substance
Economic considerations	Political considerations
Internal considerations	External considerations
Symbolic considerations	Practical considerations
Immediate future	More distant future
Ad hoc results	The relationship
Hardware	Ideology
Progress	Respect for tradition
Precedent	This case
Prestige, reputation	Results
Political points	Group welfare

Different beliefs? If I believe I'm right, and you believe you're right, we can take advantage of this difference in beliefs. We may both agree to have an impartial arbitrator settle the issue, each confident of victory. If two factions of the union leadership cannot agree on a certain wage proposal, they can agree to submit the issue to a membership vote.

Different values placed on time? You may care more about the present while the other side cares more about the future. In the language of business, you discount future value at different rates. An installment plan works on this principle. The buyer is willing to pay a higher price for a car if it is possible to pay over time; the seller is willing to accept payment later for a higher price.

Different forecasts? In a salary negotiation between an aging football star and a major team, the player may expect to win a lot of games while the team owner has the opposite expectation. Taking advantage of these different expectations, they might both agree on a modest base salary plus a big bonus if the team makes the playoffs.

Differences in aversion to risk? One last kind of difference that you may capitalize on is aversion to risk. Take, for example, the issue of deep-seabed mining that arose in international Law of the Sea negotiations. How much should mining companies pay the international community for the privilege of mining minerals from the seabed in international waters? The mining companies care more about avoiding big losses than they do about making big gains. For them deep-seabed mining is a major investment. They want to reduce the risk. The international community, on the other hand, is concerned with revenue. If some company is going to make a lot of money out of "the common heritage of mankind," the rest of the world wants a generous share.

In this difference lies the potential for a bargain advantageous to both sides. Risk can be traded for revenue. Exploiting this difference in aversion to risk, the resulting treaty provides for charging the companies low rates until they recover their investment—in other words, while their risk is high—and much higher rates thereafter, when their risk is low.

Ask for their preferences. One way to dovetail interests is to invent several options all equally acceptable to you and ask the other side which one they prefer. You want to know what is preferable, not necessarily what is acceptable. You can then take that option, work with it some more, and again present two or more variants, asking which one they prefer. In this way, without anyone's making a decision, you can improve a plan until you can find no more joint gains. For example, the agent for the sports star might ask the team owner: "What meets your interests better, a salary of $8.75 million a year for four years, or $10 million a year for three years? The latter? OK, how about between that and $7.5 million a year for three years with a $10 million bonus in each year that Fernando is voted MVP or the team wins the championship?"

If dovetailing had to be summed up in one sentence, it would be: Look for items that are of low cost to you and high benefit to them, and vice versa. Differences in interests, priorities, beliefs, forecasts, and attitudes toward risk all make dovetailing possible. A negotiator's motto could be *"Vive la différence!"*

Make their decision easy

Since success for you in a negotiation depends upon the other side's making a decision you want, you should do what you can to make that decision an easy one. Rather than make things difficult for the other side, you want to confront them with a choice that is as painless as possible. Impressed with the merits of their own case, people usually pay too little attention to ways of advancing their case by taking care of interests on the other side. To overcome the shortsightedness that results from looking too narrowly at one's immediate self-interest, you will want to put yourself in their shoes. Without some option that appeals to them, there is likely to be no agreement at all.

Whose shoes? Are you trying to influence a single negotiator, an absent boss, or some committee or other collective decision-making body? You cannot negotiate successfully with an abstraction like "Houston" or "the University of California." Instead of trying to persuade "the insurance company" to make a decision, it is wiser to focus your efforts on getting one claims agent to make a recommendation. However complex the other side's decisional process may seem, you will understand it better if you pick one person—probably the person with whom you are dealing—and see how the problem looks from his or her point of view.

By focusing on one person you are not ignoring complexities. Rather, you are handling them by understanding how they impinge on the person with whom you are negotiating. You may come to appreciate your negotiating role in a new light, and see your job, for example, as strengthening that person's hand or giving her arguments that she will need to persuade others to go along. One British ambassador described his job as "helping my opposite number get new instructions." If you place yourself firmly in the shoes of your opposite number, you will understand his problem and what kind of options might solve it.

What decision? In Chapter 2 we discussed how one can understand the other side's interests by analyzing their currently perceived choice. Now you are trying to generate options that will so change their choice that they might then decide in a way satisfactory to you. Your task is to give them not a problem but an answer, to give them not a tough decision but an easy one. It is crucial in that process to focus your attention on the content of the decision itself. That decision is often impeded by uncertainty.

Frequently you want as much as you can get, but you yourself do not know how much that is. You are likely to say, in effect, "Come up with something and I will tell you if it is enough." That may seem reasonable to you, but when you look at it from the other's point of view, you will understand the need to invent a more appealing request. For whatever they do or say, you are likely to consider that merely a floor—and ask for more. Requesting the other side to be "more forthcoming" will probably not produce a decision you want.

Many negotiators are uncertain whether they are asking for words or for performance. Yet the distinction is critical. If it is performance you want, do not add something for "negotiating room." If you want a horse to jump a fence, don't raise the fence. If you want to sell a soft drink from a vending machine for $2.00, don't mark the price at $2.50 to give yourself room to negotiate.

Most of the time you will want a promise—an agreement. Take a pencil and paper in hand and try drafting a few possible agreements. It is never too early in a negotiation to start drafting as an aid to clear thinking. Prepare multiple versions, starting with the simplest possible. What are some terms that the other party could sign, terms that would be attractive to them as well as to you? Can you reduce the number of people whose approval would be required? Can you formulate an agreement that will be easy for them to implement? The other side will take into account difficulties in carrying out an agreement; you should too.

It is usually easier, for example, to refrain from doing something not being done than to stop action already underway. And it is easier to cease doing something than to undertake an entirely new course of action. If workers want music on the job, it will be easier for the company to agree not to interfere for a few weeks with an experimental employee-run program than for the company to agree to run such a program.

Because most people are strongly influenced by their notions of legitimacy, one effective way to develop solutions easy for the other side to accept is to shape them so that they will appear legitimate. The other side is more likely to accept a solution if it seems the right thing to do—right in terms of being fair, legal, honorable, and so forth.

Few things facilitate a decision as much as precedent. Search for it. Look for a decision or statement that the other side may have made in a similar situation, and try to base a proposed agreement on it. This provides an objective standard for your request and makes it easier for them to go along. Recognizing their probable desire to be consistent, thinking about what they have already done or said will help you generate options acceptable to you that also take their point of view into account.

Making threats is not enough. In addition to the content of the decision you would like them to make, you will want to consider from their point of view the consequences of following that decision. If you were they, what results would you most fear? What would you hope for?

We often try to influence others by threats and warnings of what will happen if they do not decide as we would like. Offers are usually more effective. Concentrate both on making them aware of the consequences they can expect if they do decide as you wish and on improving those consequences from their point of view. How can you make your offers more credible? What are some specific things that they might like? Would they like to be given credit for having made the final proposal? Would they like to make the announcement? What can you invent that might be attractive to them but low in cost to yourself?

To evaluate an option from the other side's point of view, consider how they might be criticized if they adopted it. Write out a sentence or two illustrating what the other side's most powerful critic might say about the decision you are thinking of asking for. Then write out a couple of sentences with which the other side might reply in defense. Such an exercise will help you appreciate the restraints within which the other side is negotiating. It should help you generate options that will adequately meet their interests so that they can make a decision that meets yours.

A final test of an option is to write it out in the form of a "yesable proposition." Try to draft a proposal to which their responding with the single word "yes" would be sufficient, realistic, and operational. When you can do so, you will have reduced the risk that your immediate self-interest has blinded you to the necessity of meeting concerns of the other side.

In a complex situation, creative inventing is an absolute necessity. In any negotiation it may open doors and produce a range of potential agreements satisfactory to each side. Therefore, generate many options before selecting among them. Invent first; decide later. Look for shared interests and differing interests to dovetail. And seek to make their decision easy.

5   Insist on Using
Objective Criteria

However well you understand the interests of the other side, however ingeniously you invent ways of reconciling interests, however highly you value an ongoing relationship, you will almost always face the harsh reality of interests that conflict. No talk of "win-win" strategies can conceal that fact. You want the rent to be lower; the landlord wants it to be higher. You want the goods delivered tomorrow; the supplier would rather deliver them next week. You definitely prefer the large office with the view; so does your partner. Such differences cannot be swept under the rug.

Deciding on the basis of will is costly

Typically, negotiators try to resolve such conflicts by positional bargaining—in other words, by talking about what they are willing and unwilling to accept. One negotiator may demand substantive concessions simply because he insists upon them: "The price is $5,000 and that's that." Another may make a generous offer, hoping to gain approval or friendship. Whether the situation becomes a contest over who can be the most stubborn or a contest over who can be the most generous, this negotiating process focuses on what each side is willing to agree to. The outcome results from the interaction of two human wills—almost as if the negotiators were living on a desert island, with no history, no customs, and no moral standards.

As discussed in Chapter 1, trying to reconcile differences on the basis of will has serious costs. No negotiation is likely to be efficient or amicable if you pit your will against theirs, and either you have to back down or they do. And whether you are choosing a place to eat, organizing a business, or negotiating custody of a child, you are unlikely to reach a wise agreement as judged by any objective standard if you take no such standard into account.

If trying to settle differences of interest on the basis of will has such high costs, the solution is to negotiate on some basis *independent* of the will of either side—that is, on the basis of objective criteria.

The case for using objective criteria

Suppose you have entered into a fixed-price construction contract for your house that calls for reinforced concrete foundations but fails to specify how deep they should be. The contractor suggests two feet. You think five feet is closer to the usual depth for your type of house.

Now suppose the contractor says: "I went along with you on steel girders for the roof. It's your turn to go along with me on shallower foundations." No owner in his right mind would yield. Rather than horse-trade, you would insist on deciding the issue in terms of objective safety standards. "Look, maybe I'm wrong. Maybe two feet is enough. What I want are foundations strong and deep enough to hold up the building safely. Does the government have standard specifications for these soil conditions? How deep are the foundations of other buildings in this area? What is the earthquake risk here? Where do you suggest we look for standards to resolve this question?"

It is no easier to build a good contract than it is to build strong foundations. If relying on objective standards applies so clearly to a negotiation between the house owner and a contractor, why not to business deals, collective bargaining, legal settlements, and international negotiations? Why not insist that a negotiated price, for example, be based on some standard such as market value, replacement cost, depreciated book value, or competitive prices, instead of whatever the seller demands?

In short, the approach is to commit yourself to reaching a solution based on principle, not pressure. Concentrate on the merits of the problem, not the mettle of the parties. Be open to reason, but closed to threats.

Principled negotiation produces wise agreements amicably and efficiently. The more you bring standards of fairness, efficiency, or scientific merit to bear on your particular problem, the more likely you are to produce a final package that is wise and fair. The more you and the other side refer to precedent and community practice, the greater your chance of benefiting from past experience. And an agreement consistent with precedent is less vulnerable to attack. If a lease contains standard terms or if a sales contract conforms to practice in the industry, there is less risk that either negotiator will feel that he was harshly treated or will later try to repudiate the agreement.

A constant battle for dominance threatens a relationship; principled negotiation protects it. It is far easier to deal with people when both of you are discussing objective standards for settling a problem instead of trying to force each other to back down.

Approaching agreement through discussion of objective criteria also reduces the number of commitments that each side must make and then unmake as they move toward agreement. In positional bargaining, negotiators spend much of the time defending their position and attacking the other side's. People using objective criteria tend to use time more efficiently talking about possible standards and solutions.

Independent standards are even more important to efficiency when more parties are involved. In such cases positional bargaining is difficult at best. It requires coalitions among parties; and the more parties who have agreed on a position, the more difficult it becomes to change that position. Similarly, if each negotiator has a constituency or has to clear a position with a higher authority, the task of adopting positions and then changing them becomes time-consuming and difficult.

An episode during the Law of the Sea negotiations illustrates the merits of using objective criteria. At one point, India, representing the Third World bloc, proposed an initial fee for companies mining in the deep seabed of $60 million per site. The United States rejected the proposal, suggesting there be no initial fee. Both sides dug in; the matter became a contest of will.

Then someone discovered that the Massachusetts Institute of Technology (MIT) had developed a model for the economics of deep-seabed mining. This model, gradually accepted by the parties as objective, provided a way of evaluating the impact of any fee proposal on the economics of mining. When the Indian representative asked about the effect of his proposal, he was shown how the tremendous fee he proposed—payable five years before the mine would generate any revenue—would make it virtually impossible for a company to mine. Impressed, he announced that he would reconsider his position. On the other side, the MIT model helped educate the American representatives, whose information on the subject had been mostly limited to that provided by the mining companies. The model indicated that some initial fee was economically feasible. As a result, the United States also changed its position.

No one backed down; no one appeared weak—just reasonable. After a lengthy negotiation, the parties reached a tentative agreement that was mutually satisfactory.

The MIT model increased the chance of agreement and decreased costly posturing. It led to a better solution, one that would both attract companies to do mining *and* generate considerable revenue for the nations of the world. The existence of an objective model able to forecast the consequences of any proposal helped convince the parties that the tentative agreement they reached was fair. This in turn strengthened relationships among the negotiators and made it more likely an agreement would endure.*

---

* For more interesting examples from the Law of the Sea negotiations, see James K. Sebenius, *Negotiating the Law of the Sea: Lessons in the Art and Science of Reaching Agreement* (Harvard University Press, 1984).

Developing objective criteria

Carrying on a principled negotiation involves two questions: How do you develop objective criteria, and how do you use them in negotiating?

Whatever method of negotiation you use, you will do better if you prepare in advance. This certainly holds true of principled negotiation. So develop some alternative standards beforehand and think through their application to your case.

Fair standards. You will usually find more than one objective criterion available as a basis for agreement. Suppose, for example, your car is demolished and you file a claim with an insurance company. In your discussion with the adjuster, you might take into account such measures of the car's value as (1) the original cost of the car less depreciation; (2) what the car could have been sold for; (3) the standard "blue book" value for a car of that year and model; (4) what it would cost to replace that car with a comparable one; and (5) what a court might award as the value of the car.

In other cases, depending on the issue, you may wish to propose that an agreement be based upon:

Market value	What a court would decide
Precedent	Moral standards
Scientific judgment	Equal treatment
Professional standards	Tradition
Efficiency	Reciprocity
Costs	Etc.

At a minimum, objective criteria need to be independent of each side's will. Ideally, to assure a wise agreement, objective criteria should be not only independent of will but also both legitimate and practical. In a boundary dispute, for example, you may find it easier to agree on a physically salient feature such as a river than on a line three yards to the east of the riverbank.

Objective criteria should apply, at least in theory, to both sides. You can thus use the test of reciprocal application to tell you whether a proposed criterion is fair and independent of either party's will. If a real estate agency selling you a house offers a standard form contract, you would be wise to ask if that is the same standard form they use when *they* buy a house. In the international arena, the principle of self-determination is notorious for the number of peoples who insist on it as a fundamental right but deny its applicability to those on the other side. Consider the Middle East, Kashmir, or Cyprus as just three examples.

Fair procedures. To produce an outcome independent of will, you can use either fair standards for the substantive question or fair procedures for resolving the conflicting interests. Consider, for example, the age-old way to divide a piece of cake between two children: one cuts and the other chooses. Neither can complain about an unfair division.

This simple procedure was used in the Law of the Sea negotiations, one of the most complex negotiations ever undertaken. At one point, the issue of how to allocate mining sites in the deep seabed deadlocked the negotiation. Under the terms of the draft agreement, half the sites were to be mined by private companies, the other half by the Enterprise, a mining organization to be owned by the United Nations. Since the private mining companies from the rich nations had the technology and the expertise to choose the best sites, the poorer nations feared the less knowledgeable Enterprise would receive a bad bargain.

The solution devised was to agree that a private company seeking to mine the seabed would present the Enterprise with *two* proposed mining sites. The Enterprise would pick one site for itself and grant the company a license to mine the other. Since the company would not know which site it would get, it would have an incentive to make both sites as promising as possible. This simple procedure thus harnessed the company's superior expertise for mutual gain.

A variation on the procedure of "one cuts, the other chooses" is for the parties to negotiate what they think is a fair arrangement before they go on to decide their respective roles in it. In a divorce negotiation, for example, before deciding which parent will get custody of the children, the parents might agree on the visiting rights (and responsibilities) of the other parent. This gives both an incentive to agree on visitation rights each will think fair.

As you consider procedural solutions, look at other basic means of settling differences: taking turns, drawing lots, letting someone else decide, and so on.

Frequently, taking turns presents the best way for heirs to divide a large number of heirlooms left to them collectively. Afterwards, they can do some trading if they want. Or they can make the selection tentative so they see how it comes out before committing themselves to accept it. Drawing lots, flipping a coin, and other forms of chance have an inherent fairness. The results may be unequal, but each side had an equal opportunity.

Letting someone else play a key role in a joint decision is a well-established procedure with almost infinite variations. The parties can agree to submit a particular question to an expert for advice or decision. They can ask a mediator to help them reach a decision. Or they can submit the matter to an arbitrator for an authoritative and binding decision.

Professional baseball, for example, uses "last-best-offer arbitration" to settle player salary disputes. The arbitrator must choose between the last offer made by one side and the last offer made by the other. The theory is that this procedure puts pressure on the parties to make their proposals more reasonable. In baseball, and in states where this form of arbitration is compulsory for certain public employee disputes, it does seem to produce more settlements than in comparable circumstances where there is a commitment to conventional arbitration; those parties who don't settle, however, sometimes give the arbitrator an unpleasant choice between two extreme offers.

Negotiating with objective criteria

Having identified some objective criteria and procedures, how do you go about discussing them with the other side?

There are three basic points to remember:

1. Frame each issue as a joint search for objective criteria.
2. Reason and be open to reason as to which standards are most appropriate and how they should be applied.
3. Never yield to pressure, only to principle.

In short, focus on objective criteria firmly but flexibly.

Frame each issue as a joint search for objective criteria. If you are negotiating to buy a house, you might start off by saying: "Look, you want a high price and I want a low one. Let's figure out what a *fair* price would be. What objective standards might be most relevant?" You and the other side may have conflicting interests, but the two of you now have a shared goal: to determine a fair price. You might begin by suggesting one or more criteria yourself—the cost of the house adjusted for depreciation and inflation, recent sale prices of similar houses in the neighborhood, or an independent appraisal—and then invite the seller's suggestions.

Ask "What's your theory?" If the seller starts by giving you a position, such as "The price is $255,000," ask for the theory behind that price: "How did you arrive at that figure?" Treat the problem as though the seller too is looking for a fair price based on objective criteria.

Agree first on principles. Before even considering possible terms, you may want to agree on the standard or standards to apply.

Each standard the other side proposes becomes a lever you can then use to persuade them. Your case will have more impact if it is presented in terms of their criteria, and they will find it difficult to resist applying their criteria to the problem. "You say Mr. Jones sold the house next door for $260,000. Your theory is that this house should be sold for what comparable houses in the neighborhood are going for, am I right? In that case, let's look at what the house on the corner of Ellsworth and Oxford and the one at Broadway and Dana were sold for." What makes conceding particularly difficult is having to accept someone else's proposal. If they suggested the standard, their deferring to it is not an act of weakness but an act of strength, of carrying out their word.

Reason and be open to reason. What makes the negotiation a *joint* search is that, however much you may have prepared various objective criteria, you come to the table with an open mind. In most negotiations, people use precedent and other objective standards simply as arguments in support of a position. A police union might, for example, insist upon a raise of a certain amount and then justify their position with arguments about what police in other cities make. This use of standards usually only digs people even deeper into their position.

Going one step further, some people begin by announcing that their position is an issue of principle and refuse even to consider the other side's case. "It's a matter of principle" becomes a battle cry in a holy war over ideology. Practical differences escalate into principled ones, further locking in the negotiators rather than freeing them.

This is emphatically *not* what is meant by principled negotiation. Insisting that an agreement be based on objective criteria does not mean insisting that it be based solely on the criterion *you* advance. One standard of legitimacy does not preclude the existence of others. What the other side believes to be fair may not be what you believe to be fair. You should behave like a judge; although you may be predisposed to one side (in this case, your own), you should be willing to respond to reasons for applying another standard or for applying a standard differently. When each party is advancing a different standard, look for an objective basis for deciding between them, such as which standard has been used by the parties in the past or which standard is more widely applied. Just as the substantive issue itself should not be settled on the basis of will, neither should the question of which standard applies.

In a given case, there may be two standards (such as market

value and depreciated cost) that produce different results but that both parties agree seem equally legitimate. In that case, splitting the difference or otherwise compromising between the results suggested by the two objective standards is perfectly legitimate. The outcome is still independent of the will of the parties.

If, however, after a thorough discussion of the merits of an issue you still cannot accept their proposed criteria as the most appropriate, you might suggest putting them to a test. Agree on someone you both regard as fair and give him or her a list of the proposed criteria. Ask the person to decide which are the fairest or most appropriate for your situation. Since objective criteria are supposed to be legitimate and because legitimacy implies acceptance by a great many people, this is a fair thing to ask. You are not asking the third party to settle your substantive dispute — just to give you advice on what standard to use in settling it.

The difference between seeking agreement on the appropriate principles for deciding a matter and using principles simply as arguments to support positions is sometimes subtle, but always significant. A principled negotiator is open to reasoned persuasion on the merits; a positional bargainer is not. It is the combination of openness to reason with insistence on a solution based on objective criteria that makes principled negotiation so persuasive and so effective at getting the other side to play.

Never yield to pressure. Consider once again the example of negotiating with the contractor. What if he offers to hire your brother-in-law on the condition that you give in on the depth of the foundations? You would probably answer, "A job for my brother-in-law has nothing to do with whether the house will be safely supported on a foundation of that depth." What if the contractor then threatens to charge you a higher price? You would answer the same way: "We'll settle that question on the merits too. Let's see what other contractors charge for this kind of work," or "Bring me your cost figures and we'll work out a fair profit margin." If the contractor replies, "Come on, you trust me, don't you?" you would respond: "Trust is an entirely separate matter. The issue is how deep the foundations have to be to make the house safe."

Pressure can take many forms: a bribe, a threat, a manipulative appeal to trust, or a simple refusal to budge. In all these cases, the principled response is the same: invite them to state their reasoning, suggest objective criteria you think apply, and refuse to budge except on this basis. Never yield to pressure, only to principle.

Who will prevail? In any given case it is impossible to say, but in general you will have an edge. For in addition to your willpower, you also have the power of legitimacy and the persuasiveness of remaining open to reason. It will be easier for you to resist making an arbitrary concession than it will be for them to resist advancing some objective standards. A refusal to yield except in response to sound reasons is an easier position to defend—publicly and privately—than is a refusal to yield combined with a refusal to advance sound reasons.

At the least, you will usually prevail on the question of process; you can usually shift the process from positional bargaining to a search for objective criteria. In this sense principled negotiation is a dominant strategy over positional bargaining. One who insists that negotiation be based on the merits can bring others around to playing that game, since that becomes the only way to advance their substantive interests.

On substance, too, you are likely to do well. Particularly for those who might otherwise be browbeaten by a positional bargainer, principled negotiation allows you to hold your own and still be fair. Principle serves as your hardhearted partner who will not let you yield to pressure. It is a form of "right makes might."

If the other side truly will not budge and will not advance a persuasive basis for their position, then there is no further negotiation. You now have a choice like the one you face when you walk into a store that has a fixed, nonnegotiable price on what you want to buy. You can take it or leave it. Before leaving it you should see if you have overlooked some objective standard that makes their offer a fair one. If you find such a standard and if you would rather reach agreement on that basis than have no agreement, do so. The availability of that relevant standard avoids the cost of giving in to an arbitrary position.

If there is no give in their position and you find no principled basis for accepting it, you should assess what you might gain by accepting their unjustified position rather than going to your best alternative. You should weigh that substantive benefit against the benefit to your reputation as a principled negotiator that could come from walking away.

Shifting discussion in a negotiation from the question of what the other side is willing to do to the question of how the matter ought to be decided does not end argument, nor does it guarantee a favorable result. It does, however, provide a strategy you can vigorously pursue without the high costs of positional bargaining.

"It's company policy"

Let's look at a real case where one party used positional bargaining and the other principled negotiation. Tom, one of our colleagues, had his parked car totally destroyed by a dump truck. The car was covered by insurance, but the exact amount Tom could recover remained for him to work out with the insurance adjuster.

Insurance Adjuster	Tom
We have studied your case and we have decided the policy applies. That means you're entitled to a settlement of $13,600.	
	I see. How did you reach that figure?
That's how much we decided the car was worth.	
	I understand, but what standard did you use to determine that amount? Do you know where I can buy a comparable car for that much?

Insurance Adjuster	**Tom**
How much are you asking for?	
	Whatever I'm entitled to under the policy. I found a secondhand car just about like it for $17,700. Adding the sales and excise tax, it would come to about $19,000.
$19,000! That's too much!	
	I'm not asking for $19,000 or $18,000 or $20,000, but for fair compensation. Do you agree that it's only fair I get enough to replace the car?
OK, I'll offer you $15,000. That's the highest I can go. Company policy.	
	How does the company figure that?
Look, $15,000 is all you'll get. Take it or leave it.	
	$15,000 may be fair. I don't know. I certainly understand your position if you're bound by company policy. But unless you can state objectively why that amount is what I'm *entitled* to, I think I'll do better in court. Why don't we study the matter and talk again? Is Wednesday at eleven a good time to talk?

.   .   .

OK, Mr. Griffith, I've got an ad here in today's paper offering a car exactly the same make, model, and year as yours for $14,800.	
	I see. What does it say about the mileage?
49,000. Why?	
	Because mine only had 25,000 miles. How many dollars does that increase the worth in your book?

Insurance Adjuster	**Tom**
Let me see . . . $1,650.	Assuming the $14,800 as one possible base, that brings the figure to $16,450. Does the ad specify the technology package?
No.	How much extra for that in your book?
$1,100.	How about an autodimming mirror?

. . .

A half hour later Tom walked out with a check for $18,024.

III YES, BUT . . .

6 What If They Are More Powerful?

(Develop Your BATNA —
Best Alternative To a Negotiated Agreement)

Of what use is talking about interests, options, and standards if the other side has a stronger bargaining position? What do you do if the other side is richer or better connected, or if they have a larger staff or more powerful weapons?

No method can guarantee success if all the leverage lies on the other side. No book on gardening can teach you to grow lilies in a desert or a cactus in a swamp. If you enter an antique store to buy a sterling silver George IV tea set worth thousands of dollars and all you have is one hundred-dollar bill, you should not expect skillful negotiation to overcome the difference. In any negotiation there exist realities that are hard to change. In response to power, the most any method of negotiation can do is to meet two objectives: *first,* to protect you against making an agreement you should reject and *second,* to help you make the most of the assets you do have so that any agreement you reach will satisfy your interests as well as possible. Let's take each objective in turn.

Protecting yourself

When you are trying to catch an airplane your goal may seem tremendously important; looking back on it, you see you could have caught the next plane. Negotiation will often present you with a similar situation. You will worry, for instance, about failing to reach agreement on an important business deal in which you have invested a great deal of yourself. Under these conditions, a major danger is that you will be too accommodating to the views of the other side—too quick to go along. The siren song of "Let's all agree and put an end to this" becomes persuasive. You may end up with a deal you should have rejected.

The costs of using a bottom line. Negotiators commonly try to protect themselves against such an outcome by establishing in advance the worst acceptable outcome—their "bottom line." If you are buying, a bottom line is the highest price you would pay. If you are selling, a bottom line is the lowest amount you would accept. You and your spouse might, for example, ask $300,000 for your house and agree between yourselves to accept no offer below $260,000.

Having a bottom line makes it easier to resist pressure and temptations of the moment. In the house example, it might be impossible for a buyer to pay more than $244,000, and everyone involved may know that you bought the house not so long ago for only $235,000. In this situation, where you have the power to produce agreement and the buyer does not, the brokers and anyone else in the room may turn to you. Your predetermined bottom line may save you from making a decision you would later regret.

If there is more than one person on your side, jointly adopting a bottom line helps ensure that no one will indicate to the other side that you might settle for less. It limits the authority of a lawyer, broker, or other agent. "Get the best price you can, but you are not authorized to sell for less than $260,000," you might say. If your side is a loose coalition of newspaper unions negotiating with an association of publishers, agreement on a bottom line reduces the risk that one union will be split off by offers from the other side.

But the protection afforded by adopting a bottom line involves high costs. It limits your ability to benefit from what you learn during negotiation. By definition, a bottom line is a position that is not to be changed. To that extent you have shut your ears, deciding in advance that nothing the other party says could cause you to raise or lower that bottom line.

A bottom line also inhibits imagination. It reduces the incentive to invent a tailor-made solution that would reconcile differing interests in a way more advantageous for both you and them. Almost every negotiation involves more than one variable. Rather than simply selling your place for $260,000, you might serve your interests better by settling for $235,000 with a first refusal on resale, a delayed closing, the right to use the barn for storage for two years, and an option to buy back two acres of the pasture. If you insist on a bottom line, you are not likely to explore an imaginative solution like this. A bottom line—by its very nature rigid—is almost certain to be *too* rigid.

Moreover, a bottom line is likely to be set too high. Suppose you are sitting around the breakfast table with your family trying to decide the lowest price you should accept for your house. One family member suggests $200,000. Another replies, "We should get at least $240,000." A third chimes in, "$240,000 for *our* house? That would be a steal. It's worth at least $300,000." Who sitting at the table will object, knowing they will benefit from a higher price? Once decided upon, such a bottom line may be hard to change and may prevent your selling the house when you should. Under other circumstances a bottom line may be too low; rather than selling at such a figure, you would have been better off renting.

In short, while adopting a bottom line may protect you from accepting a very bad agreement, it may keep you both from inventing and from agreeing to a solution it would be wise to accept. An arbitrarily selected figure is no measure of what you should accept.

Is there an alternative to the bottom line? Is there a measure for agreements that will protect you against both accepting an agreement you should reject and rejecting an agreement you should accept? There is.

Know your BATNA. When a family is deciding on the minimum price for their house, the right question for them to ask is not what they "ought" to be able to get, but what they will do if by a certain time they have not sold the house. Will they keep it on the market indefinitely? Will they rent it, tear it down, turn the land into a parking lot, let someone else live in it rent-free on condition they paint it, or what? Which of those alternatives is most attractive, all things considered? And how does that alternative compare with the best offer received for the house? It may be that one of those alternatives is more attractive than selling the house for $260,000. On the other hand, selling the house for as little as $224,000 may be better than holding on to it indefinitely. It is most unlikely that any arbitrarily selected bottom line truly reflects the family's interests.

The reason you negotiate is to produce something better than the results you can obtain without negotiating. What are those results? What is that alternative? What is your BATNA—your Best Alternative To a Negotiated Agreement? *That* is the standard against which any proposed agreement should be measured. That is the only standard that can protect you both from accepting terms that are too unfavorable and from rejecting terms it would be in your interest to accept.

Your BATNA not only is a better measure but also has the advantage of being flexible enough to permit the exploration of imaginative solutions. Instead of ruling out any solution that does not meet your bottom line, you can compare a proposal with your BATNA to see whether it better satisfies your interests.

The insecurity of an unknown BATNA. If you have not thought carefully about what you will do if you fail to reach an agreement, you are negotiating with your eyes closed. You may, for instance, be too optimistic and assume that you have many other choices: other houses for sale, other buyers for your secondhand car, other plumbers, other jobs available, other wholesalers, and so on. Even when your alternative is fixed, you may be taking too rosy a view of the consequences of not reaching agreement. You may not be appreciating the full agony of a lawsuit, a contested divorce, a strike, an arms race, or a war.

One frequent mistake is psychologically to see your alternatives in the aggregate. You may be telling yourself that if you do not reach agreement on a salary for this job, you could always go to California, or go south, or go back to school, or write, or work on a farm, or live in Paris, or do something else. In your mind you are likely to find the sum of these alternatives more attractive than working for a specific salary in a particular job. The difficulty is that you cannot have the sum total of all those other alternatives; if you fail to reach agreement, you will have to choose just one.

In most circumstances, however, the greater danger is that you are *too* committed to reaching agreement. Not having developed any alternative to a negotiated solution, you are unduly pessimistic about what would happen if negotiations broke off.

As valuable as knowing your BATNA may be, you may hesitate to explore alternatives. You hope this buyer or the next will make you an attractive offer for the house. You may avoid facing the question of what you will do if no agreement is reached. You may think to yourself, "Let's negotiate first and see what happens. If things don't work out, then I'll figure out what to do." But having at least a tentative answer to the question is absolutely essential if you are to conduct your negotiations wisely. Whether you should or should not agree on something in a negotiation depends entirely upon the attractiveness to you of the best available alternative.

Formulate a trip wire. Although your BATNA is the true measure by which you should judge any proposed agreement, you may want another test as well. To give you early warning that the content of a possible agreement is beginning to run the risk of being too unattractive, it is useful to identify one far from perfect agreement that is better than your BATNA. Before accepting any agreement worse than this trip-wire package, you should take a break and reexamine the situation. Like a bottom line, a trip wire can limit the authority of an agent. "Don't sell for less than $258,000, the price I paid plus interest, until you've talked to me."

A trip wire should provide you with some margin in reserve. If after reaching the standard reflected in your trip wire you decide to call in a mediator, you have left him with something on your side to work with. You still have some room to move.

Making the most of your assets

Protecting yourself against a bad agreement is one thing. Making the most of the assets you have to produce a good agreement is another. How do you do this? Again the answer lies in your BATNA.

The better your BATNA, the greater your power. People think of negotiating power as being determined by resources like wealth, political connections, physical strength, friends, and military might. In fact, the relative negotiating power of two parties depends primarily upon how attractive to each is the option of not reaching agreement.

Consider a wealthy tourist who wants to buy a small brass pot for a modest price from a vendor at the Mumbai railroad station. The vendor may be poor, but she is likely to know the market. If she does not sell the pot to this tourist, she can sell it to another. From her experience she can estimate when and for how much she could sell it to someone else. The tourist may be wealthy and "powerful," but in this negotiation he will be weak indeed unless he knows approximately how much it would cost and how difficult it would be to find a comparable pot elsewhere. He is almost certain either to miss his chance to buy such a pot or to pay too high a price. The tourist's wealth in no way strengthens his negotiating power. If apparent, it *weakens* his ability to buy the pot at a low price. To convert that wealth into negotiating power, the tourist would have to apply it to learn about the price at which he could buy an equally or more attractive brass pot somewhere else.

Think for a moment about how you would feel walking into a job interview with no other job offers—only some uncertain leads. Think how the talk about salary would go. Now contrast that with how you would feel walking in with two other job offers. How would that salary negotiation proceed? The difference is power.

What is true for negotiations between individuals is equally true for negotiations between organizations. The relative negotiating power of a large industry and a small town trying to raise taxes on a factory is determined not by the relative size of their respective budgets, or their political clout, but by each side's best alternative. In one case, a small town negotiated a company with a factory just outside the town limits from a "goodwill" payment of $300,000 a year to one of $2,300,000 a year. How?

The town knew exactly what it would do if no agreement was reached: It would expand the town limits to include the factory and then tax the factory the full residential rate of some $2,500,000 a year. The corporation had committed itself to keeping the factory; it had developed no alternative to reaching agreement. At first glance the corporation seemed to have a great deal of power. It provided most of the jobs in the town, which was suffering economically; a factory shutdown or relocation would devastate the town. And the taxes the corporation was already paying helped provide the salaries of the very town leaders who were demanding more. Yet all of these assets, because they were not converted into a good BATNA, proved of little use. Having an attractive BATNA, the small town had more ability to affect the outcome of the negotiation than did one of the world's largest corporations.

Develop your BATNA. Vigorous exploration of what you will do if you do not reach agreement can greatly strengthen your hand. Attractive alternatives are not just sitting there waiting for you; you usually have to develop them. Generating possible BATNAs requires three distinct operations: (1) inventing a list of actions you might conceivably take if no agreement is reached; (2) improving some of the more promising ideas and converting them into practical alternatives; and (3) selecting, tentatively, the one alternative that seems best.

The first operation is inventing. If, by the end of the month, Company X does not make you a satisfactory job offer, what are some things you might do? Take a job with Company Y? Look in another city? Start a business on your own? What else? For a labor union, alternatives to a negotiated agreement would presumably include calling a strike, working without a contract, giving a sixty-day notice of a strike, asking for a mediator, and calling on union members to "work to rule."

The second stage is to improve the best of your ideas and turn the most promising into real alternatives. If you are thinking about working in Chicago, try to turn that idea into at least one job offer there. With a Chicago job offer in hand (or even having discovered that you are unable to produce one) you are much better prepared to assess the merits of a New York offer. While a labor union is still negotiating, it should convert the ideas of calling in a mediator and of striking into drafts of specific operational decisions ready for execution. The union might, for instance, take a vote of its membership to authorize a strike if a settlement is not achieved by the time the contract expires.

The final step in developing a BATNA is selecting the best among the alternatives. If you do not reach agreement in the negotiations, which of your realistic alternatives do you now plan to pursue?

Having gone through this effort, you now have a BATNA. Judge every offer against it. The better your BATNA, the greater your ability to improve the terms of any negotiated agreement. Knowing what you are going to do if the negotiation does not lead to agreement will give you additional confidence in the negotiating process. It is easier to break off negotiations if you know where you're going. The greater your willingness to break off negotiations, the more forcefully you can present your interests and the basis on which you believe an agreement should be reached.

The desirability of disclosing your BATNA to the other side depends upon your assessment of the other side's thinking. If your BATNA is extremely attractive—if you have another customer waiting in the next room—it is in your interest to let the other side know. If they think you lack a good alternative when in fact you have one, then you should almost certainly let them know. However, if your best alternative to a negotiated agreement is worse for you than they think, disclosing it will weaken rather than strengthen your hand.

Consider the other side's BATNA. You should also think about the alternatives to a negotiated agreement available to the other side. The more you can learn of their alternatives, the better prepared you are for negotiation. Knowing their alternatives, you can realistically estimate what you can expect from the negotiation.

They may be unduly optimistic about what they can do if no agreement is reached. Perhaps they have a vague notion that they have a great many alternatives and are under the influence of their cumulative total. If they appear to overestimate their BATNA, you will want to help them think through whether their expectations are realistic.

Their BATNA may be better for them than any fair solution you can imagine. Suppose you are a community group concerned about the potential noxious gases to be emitted by a power plant now under construction. The power company's BATNA is either to ignore your protests altogether or to keep you talking while they finish building the plant. To get them to take your concerns seriously, you may have to file a lawsuit seeking to have their construction permit revoked. In other words, if their BATNA is so good they don't see any need to negotiate on the merits, consider what you can do to change it.

If both sides have attractive BATNAs, the best outcome of the negotiation—for both parties—may well be not to reach agreement. In such cases a successful negotiation is one in which you and they amicably and efficiently discover that the best way to advance your respective interests is for each of you to look elsewhere and not to try further to reach agreement.

When the other side is powerful

If the other side has big guns, you do not want to turn a negotiation into a gunfight. The stronger they appear in terms of physical or economic power, the more you benefit by negotiating on the merits. To the extent that they have muscle and you have principle, the larger a role you can establish for principle the better off you are.

Having a good BATNA can help you negotiate on the merits. You can convert such resources as you have into effective negotiating power by developing and improving your BATNA. Apply knowledge, time, money, people, connections, and wits into devising the best solution for you independent of the other side's assent. The more easily and happily you can walk away from a negotiation, the greater your capacity to affect its outcome.

Developing your BATNA thus not only enables you to determine what is a minimally acceptable agreement, it will probably raise that minimum. Developing your BATNA is perhaps the most effective course of action you can take in dealing with a seemingly more powerful negotiator.

7 What If They Won't Play?

(Use Negotiation Jujitsu)

Talking about interests, options, and standards may be a wise, efficient, and amicable game, but what if the other side won't play? While you try to discuss interests, they may state their position in unequivocal terms. You may be concerned with developing possible agreements to maximize the gains of both parties. They may be attacking your proposals, concerned only with maximizing their own gains. You may attack the problem on its merits; they may attack you. What can you do to turn them away from positions and toward the merits?

There are three basic approaches for focusing their attention on the merits. The first centers on what *you* can do. You yourself can concentrate on the merits, rather than on positions. This method, the subject of this book, is contagious; it holds open the prospect of success to those who will talk about interests, options, and criteria. In effect, you can change the game simply by starting to play a new one.

If this doesn't work and they continue to use positional bargaining, you can resort to a second strategy that focuses on what *they* may do. It counters the basic moves of positional bargaining in ways that direct their attention to the merits. This strategy we call *negotiation jujitsu*.

The third approach focuses on what a *third party* can do. If neither principled negotiation nor negotiation jujitsu gets them to play, consider including a third party trained to focus the discussion on interests, options, and criteria. Perhaps the most effective

tool a third party can use in such an effort is the one-text mediation procedure.

The first approach—principled negotiation—has already been
discussed. Negotiation jujitsu and the one-text procedure are explained in this chapter. The chapter ends with a dialogue based
on an actual landlord-tenant negotiation that illustrates in detail
how you might persuade an unwilling party to play, using a combination of principled negotiation and negotiation jujitsu.

Negotiation jujitsu

If the other side announces a firm position, you may be tempted
to criticize and reject it. If they criticize your proposal, you may
be tempted to defend it and dig yourself in. If they attack you,
you may be tempted to defend yourself and counterattack. In
short, if they push you hard, you will tend to push back.

Yet if you do, you will end up playing the positional bargaining game. Rejecting their position only locks them in. Defending
your proposal only locks *you* in. And defending yourself side-
tracks the negotiation into a clash of personalities. You will find
yourself in a vicious cycle of attack and defense, and you will
waste a lot of time and energy in useless pushing and pulling.

If pushing back does not work, what does? How can you prevent the cycle of action and reaction? *Do not push back.* When
they assert their positions, do not reject them. When they attack
your ideas, don't defend them. When they attack you, don't counterattack. Break the vicious cycle by refusing to react. Instead of
pushing back, sidestep their attack and deflect it against the problem. As in the Oriental martial arts of judo and jujitsu, avoid pit-
ting your strength against theirs directly; instead, use your skill to
step aside and turn their strength to your ends. Rather than resisting their force, channel it into exploring interests, inventing options for mutual gain, and searching for independent standards.

How does "negotiation jujitsu" work in practice? How do you
sidestep their attack and deflect it against the problem?

Typically their "attack" will consist of three maneuvers: asserting their position forcefully, attacking your ideas, and attacking you. Let's consider how a principled negotiator can deal with each of these.

Don't attack their position, look behind it. When the other side sets forth their position, neither reject it nor accept it. Treat it as one possible option. Look for the interests behind it, seek out the principles that it reflects, and think about ways to improve it.

Let's say you represent an association of teachers striking for higher pay and for seniority as the only criterion in layoffs. The school board has proposed a $2,000 raise across the board plus retention of the right to decide unilaterally who gets laid off. Mine their position for the interests that lie below the surface. "What exactly are the budget trade-offs involved in raising the salary schedule more than $2,000?" "Why do you feel a need to maintain complete control over layoffs?"

Assume every position they take is a genuine attempt to address the basic concerns of each side; ask them how they think it addresses the problem at hand. Treat their position as one option and objectively examine the extent to which it meets the interests of each party, or might be improved to do so. "How will a $2,000 across-the-board increase keep our schools' salaries competitive with others in the area and thus assure that the students will have high-quality teachers?" "How could you satisfy the teachers that your evaluation procedure for layoffs would be fair? We believe that you personally would be fair, but what would happen if you left? How can we leave our livelihoods and our families' wellbeing up to a potentially arbitrary decision?"

Seek out and discuss the principles underlying the other side's positions. "What is the theory that makes $2,000 a fair salary increase? Is it based on what other schools pay or what others with comparable qualifications make?" "Do you believe that the town's least experienced teachers should be laid off first or the most experienced—who, of course, have higher salaries?"

To direct their attention toward improving the options on the table, discuss with them hypothetically what would happen if one of their positions was accepted. In 1970, an American lawyer had a chance to interview President Gamal Abdel Nasser of Egypt on the subject of the Arab-Israeli conflict. He asked Nasser, "What do you want [Israel's Prime Minister] Golda Meir to do?"

Nasser replied, "Withdraw!"

"Withdraw?" the lawyer asked.

"Withdraw from every inch of Arab territory!"

"Without a deal? With nothing from you?" the American asked incredulously.

"Nothing. It's our territory. She should promise to withdraw," Nasser replied.

The American asked, "What would happen to Golda Meir if tomorrow morning she appeared on Israeli radio and television and said, 'On behalf of the people of Israel, I hereby promise to withdraw from every inch of territory occupied in 1967: the Sinai Peninsula, the Gaza Strip, the West Bank, Jerusalem, the Golan Heights. And I want you to know, I have no commitment of any kind from any Arab whatsoever.'"

Nasser burst out laughing. "Oh, would *she* have trouble at home!"

Understanding what an unrealistic option Egypt had been offering Israel may have contributed to Nasser's stated willingness later that day to accept a cease-fire in the ongoing hostilities.

Don't defend your ideas, invite criticism and advice. A lot of time in negotiation is spent criticizing. Rather than resisting the other side's criticism, invite it. Instead of asking them to accept or reject an idea, ask them what's wrong with it. "What concerns of yours would this salary proposal fail to take into account?" Examine their negative judgments to find out their underlying interests and to improve your ideas from their point of view. Rework your ideas in light of what you learn from them, and thus turn criticism from an obstacle in the process of working toward agreement into an essential ingredient of that process. "If I understand you, you're saying you can't afford to give 750 teachers more than a $2,000 across-the-board raise. What if we accept that with the stipulation that any money saved by hiring fewer than 750 full-time teachers will be distributed as a monthly bonus to those teachers who are working?"

Another way to channel criticism in a constructive direction is to turn the situation around and ask for their advice. Ask them what they would do if they were in your position. "If your jobs were at stake, what would you do? Our members are feeling so insecure about their jobs and frustrated by their shrinking dollars they're talking about inviting a militant union in to represent them. If you were leading this association, how would you act?" Thus, you lead them to confront your half of the problem. In doing so, they may be able to invent a solution that meets your concerns. "Part of the problem here seems to be that the teachers feel no one's listening. Would it help to have regular sessions at which teachers could meet with the school board?"

Recast an attack on you as an attack on the problem. When the other side attacks you personally—as frequently happens—resist the temptation to defend yourself or to attack them. Instead, sit back and allow them to let off steam. Listen to them, show you understand what they are saying, and when they have finished, recast their attack on you as an attack on the problem. "When you say that a strike shows we don't care about the children, I hear your concern about the children's education. I want you to know that we share this concern: they are our children and our students. We want the strike to end so we can go back to educating them. What can we both do now to reach an agreement as quickly as possible?"

Ask questions and pause. Those engaged in negotiation jujitsu use two key tools. The first is to use questions instead of statements. Statements generate resistance, whereas questions generate answers. Questions allow the other side to get their points across and let you understand them. They pose challenges and can be used to lead the other side to confront the problem. Questions offer them no target to strike at, no position to attack. Questions do not criticize, they educate. "Do you think it would be better to have teachers cooperating in a process they felt they were participating in, or actively resisting one they felt was imposed on them and failed to take their concerns into account?"

Silence is one of your best weapons. Use it. If they have made an unreasonable proposal or an attack you regard as unjustified, the best thing to do may be to sit there and not say a word.

If you have asked an honest question to which they have provided an insufficient answer, just wait. People tend to feel uncomfortable with silence, particularly if they have doubts about the merits of something they have said. For example, if a teacher's representative asks, "Why shouldn't teachers have a say in layoff policy?" the school board chairman might find himself at a loss: "Layoffs are a purely administrative matter. . . . Well, of course teachers have an interest in layoff policy, but they really aren't the best qualified to know who's a good teacher. . . . Uh, what I mean is . . . ."

Silence often creates the impression of a stalemate that the other side will feel impelled to break by answering your question or coming up with a new suggestion. When you ask questions, pause. Don't take them off the hook by going right on with another question or some comment of your own. Some of the most effective negotiating you will ever do is when you are not talking.

Consider the one-text procedure

You will probably call in a third party only if your own efforts to shift the game from positional bargaining to principled negotiation have failed. The problem you face may be illustrated by a simple story of a negotiation between a husband and wife who plan to build a new house.

The wife is thinking of a two-story house with a chimney and a bay window. The husband is thinking of a modern one-story ranch-style house with a den and a garage with a lot of storage space. In the process of negotiating, each asks the other a number of questions, like "What are your views on the living room?" and "Do you really insist on having it your way?" Through answering such questions, two separate plans become more and more fixed. They each ask an architect to prepare first a sketch and then more detailed plans, ever more firmly digging themselves into their respective positions. In response to the wife's demand for some flexibility, the husband agrees to reduce the length of the garage by one foot. In response to his insistence on a concession, the wife agrees to give up a back porch, which she says she had always wanted but which did not even appear on her plan. Each argues in support of one plan and against the other. In the process, feelings are hurt and communication becomes difficult. Neither side wants to make a concession, since it will likely lead only to requests for more concessions.

This is a classic case of positional bargaining. If you cannot change the process to one of seeking a solution on the merits, perhaps a third party can. More easily than one of those directly involved, a mediator can separate the people from the problem and direct the discussion to interests and options. Further, he or she can often suggest some impartial basis for resolving differences. A third party can also separate inventing from decision-making, reduce the number of decisions required to reach agreement, and help the parties know what they will get when they do decide. One process designed to enable a third party to do all this is known as the *one-text procedure*.

In the house-designing negotiation between husband and wife, an independent architect is called in and shown the latest plans reflecting the present positions of the husband and the wife. Not all third parties will behave wisely. One architect, for example, might ask the parties for clarification of their positions, press them for a long series of concessions, and make them even more emotionally attached to their particular solutions. But an architect using the one-text procedure would behave differently. Rather than ask about their positions he asks about their interests: not how big a bay window the wife wants, but why she wants it. "Is it for morning sun or afternoon sun? Is it to look out or look in?" He would ask the husband, "Why do you want a garage? What things do you need to store? What do you expect to do in your den? Read? Look at television? Entertain friends? When will you use the den? During the day? Weekends? Evenings?" And so forth.

The architect makes clear he is not asking either spouse to give up a position. Rather, he is exploring the possibility that he might be able to make a recommendation to them—but even that is uncertain. At this stage he is just trying to learn all he can about their needs and interests.

Afterward, the architect develops a list of interests and needs of the two spouses ("morning sun, open fireplace, comfortable place to read, room for a wood shop, storage for snow-blower and medium-size car," and so on). He asks each spouse in turn to criticize the list and suggest improvements on it. It is hard to make concessions, but it is easy to criticize.

A few days later the architect returns with a rough floor plan. "Personally, I am dissatisfied with it, but before working on it further I thought I would get your criticisms. What would be wrong with something like this?" The husband might say, "What's wrong with it? Well, for one thing, the bathroom is too far from the bedroom. I don't see enough room for my books. And where would overnight guests sleep?" The wife is similarly asked for her criticism of the first sketch.

A short time later the architect comes back with a second sketch, again asking for criticism. "I've tried to deal with the bathroom problem and the book problem, and also with the idea of using the den as a spare bedroom and adding more storage space. What do you think about this?" As the plan takes shape, each spouse will tend to raise those issues most important to him or to her, not trivial details. Without conceding anything, the wife, for example, will want to make sure that the architect fully understands her major needs. No one's ego, not even that of the architect, is committed to any draft. Inventing the best possible reconciliation of their interests within their financial constraints is separated from making decisions and is free of the fear of making an overhasty commitment. Husband and wife do not have to abandon their positions, but they now sit side by side, at least figuratively, jointly critiquing the plans as they take shape and helping the architect prepare a recommendation he may later present to them.

And so it goes, through a third plan, a fourth, and a fifth. Finally, when he feels he can improve it no further, the architect says, "This is the best I can do. I have tried to reconcile your various interests as best I could. Many of the issues I have resolved using standard architectural and engineering solutions, precedent, and the best professional judgment I can bring to bear. Here it is. I recommend you accept this plan."

Each spouse now has only one decision to make: yes or no. In making their decisions they know exactly what they are going to get. And a yes answer can be made contingent on the other side's also saying yes. The one-text procedure not only shifts the game away from positional bargaining, it greatly simplifies the process both of inventing options and of deciding jointly on one.

In other negotiations, who could play the role of the architect? You could invite a third party in to mediate. Or, in negotiations involving more than two parties, a natural third party may be a participant whose interests on this issue lie more in effecting an agreement than in affecting the particular terms.

In many negotiations that someone may be you. For instance, you may be a sales representative for a plastics plant negotiating a large order with an industrial customer who makes plastic bottles. The customer may want a special kind of plastic made up, but the plant you represent may be reluctant to do the retooling needed for the order. Your commission depends more on effecting an agreement between your customer and your production people than on affecting the terms. Or you may be a legislative assistant for a senator who is more concerned with getting a certain appropriations bill passed than with whether the appropriation is ten million dollars or eleven. Or you may be a manager trying to decide an issue on which each of your two subordinates favors a different course of action; you care more about making a decision both can live with than about which alternative is chosen. In each of these cases, even though you are an active participant, it may be in your best interest to behave as a mediator would and to use the one-text procedure. Mediate your own dispute.

Perhaps the most famous use of the one-text procedure was by the United States at the Camp David summit in September 1978 when mediating between Egypt and Israel. The United States listened to both sides, prepared a draft to which no one was committed, asked for criticism, and improved the draft again and again until the mediators felt they could improve it no further. After thirteen days and some twenty-three drafts, the United States had a text it was prepared to recommend. When President Jimmy Carter finally did recommend it, Israel and Egypt accepted. As a mechanical technique for limiting the number of decisions, reducing the uncertainty of each decision, and preventing the parties from getting increasingly locked into their positions, it worked remarkably well.

The one-text procedure is a great help for two-party negotiations involving a mediator. It is almost essential for large multilateral negotiations. One hundred and fifty nations, for example, cannot constructively discuss a hundred and fifty different proposals. Nor can they make concessions contingent upon mutual concessions by everybody else. Combining parts of many different proposals is also unlikely to produce the best answer, as illustrated by the old quip that a camel is a horse designed by a committee. Multiple parties need some way to simplify the process of decision-making without diminishing the quality of the outcome. The one-text procedure serves that purpose.

The Law of the Sea negotiations started making significant progress only when they began using a prototype of the one-text procedure created by veteran diplomat Tommy Koh of Singapore. The negotiators were divided into groups to work on different issues with appointed chairpersons tabling drafts, soliciting criticism, and revising drafts within each group. A similar process was used for parts of the South African constitutional negotiations that ultimately ended apartheid and created an inclusive multilateral democracy.*

Note that in most situations you do not have to get anyone's consent to start using the one-text procedure. Simply prepare a draft and ask for criticism. Again, you can change the game simply by starting to play the new one. Even if the other side is not willing to talk to you directly (or vice versa), a third party can take a draft around.

Getting them to play:
The case of Jones Realty and Frank Turnbull

The following real-life example of a negotiation between a landlord and tenant should give you a feel for how you might deal with a party who is reluctant to engage in principled negotiation. It illustrates what it means to change the game by starting to play a new one.

The case in brief. Frank Turnbull rented an apartment in March from Jones Realty for $1,200 a month. In July, when he and his roommate, Paul, wanted to move out, Turnbull learned that the apartment was under rent control. The maximum legal rent was $932 a month—$268 less than he had been paying.

Disturbed that he had been overcharged, Turnbull called on Mrs. Jones of Jones Realty to discuss the problem. At first, Mrs. Jones was unreceptive and hostile. She claimed to be right and accused Turnbull of ingratitude and blackmail. After several long negotiating sessions, however, Mrs. Jones agreed to reimburse Turnbull and his roommate. Her tone in the end became friendlier and apologetic.

---

*Interestingly, in South Africa the facilitators using the one-text process were talented members of the South African business community. While the business community was hardly neutral, everyone understood that its overriding interest was to maintain stability and prosperity and avoid a civil war, interests likely to be best served by a successful process.

Throughout, Turnbull used the method of principled negotiation. Presented below is a selection of the exchanges that took place during the negotiation. Each exchange is headed by a stock phrase that a principled negotiator might use in any similar situation. Following each exchange is an analysis of the theory that lies behind it and its impact.

"Please correct me if I'm wrong"

Turnbull: Mrs. Jones, I've just learned—please correct me if I'm wrong—that our apartment's under rent control. We've been told that the legal maximum rent is $932 a month. Have we been misinformed?

Analysis. The essence of principled negotiation lies in remaining open to persuasion by objective facts and principles. By cautiously treating his view of the objective facts as possibly inaccurate and asking Mrs. Jones to correct it, Turnbull establishes a dialogue based on reason. He invites her to participate by either agreeing with the facts as presented or setting them right. This approach makes them two colleagues trying to establish the facts. The confrontation is defused. If Turnbull simply asserted his views of the facts as facts, Mrs. Jones would feel disrespected, threatened, and defensive. She might deny the facts, especially if she thought any aspect of Turnbull's view was inaccurate or incomplete. The negotiation would not start off constructively.

If Turnbull is genuinely mistaken, asking for corrections beforehand will make them easier to accept. To tell Mrs. Jones that these are the facts, only to learn he is wrong, would make him lose face. Worse yet, she would then doubt all the more anything else he says, making it difficult to negotiate.

Making yourself open to correction and persuasion is a pillar in the strategy of principled negotiation. You can convince the other side to be open to the principles and objective standards you suggest only if you show yourself open to the ones they suggest.

"We appreciate what you've done for us"

Turnbull: Paul and I understand you were doing a personal favor by renting us this apartment. You were very kind to put in the time and effort, and we appreciate it.

Analysis. Giving personal support to the person on the other side is crucial to disentangling the people from the problem—separating relationship issues from the substantive merits. By expressing his appreciation of Mrs. Jones's good deeds, Turnbull in effect says, "We have nothing against you personally. We think you're a generous person." He puts himself on her side. He defuses any threat she may feel to her self-image.

Praise and support, moreover, imply that the person will continue to deserve them. After being praised, Mrs. Jones now has a slight emotional investment in Turnbull's approval of her. She has something to lose and as a result may act more conciliatory.

"Our concern is fairness"

Turnbull: We want to know that we didn't pay any more than we should have. When we're persuaded that the rent paid measures up fairly to the time spent in the apartment, we'll call it even and move out.

Analysis. Turnbull takes a basic stand on principle and announces his intention to stick to it; he must be persuaded on the basis of principle. At the same time, he lets Mrs. Jones know he is open to persuasion along the lines of this principle. She is thus left with little choice but to reason with him in pursuit of her interests.

Turnbull does not take a righteous stand on principle backed up with whatever power he possesses. Not only are his ends principled but also the means he contemplates. His ends, he claims, are a fair balance between rent paid and time spent. If convinced the rent paid is just right for the time spent, he will move out. If the rent paid is excessive, it is only fair that he remain in the apartment until the rent and the time spent are in balance.

"We would like to settle this on the basis of independent standards, not of who can do what to whom"

Mrs. Jones: It's funny you should mention fairness, because what you're really saying is that you and Paul just want money, and that you're going to take advantage of your still being in the apartment to try and get it from us. That really makes me angry. If I had my way, you and Paul would be out of the apartment today.

Turnbull *(barely controlling his anger):* I must not be making myself clear. Of course it would be nice if Paul and I got some money. Of course we could try and stay here in the apartment until you got us evicted. But that's not the point, Mrs. Jones.

More important to us than making a few dollars here or there is the feeling of being treated fairly. No one likes to feel cheated. And if we made this a matter of who's got the power and refused to move, we'd have to go to court, waste a lot of time and money, and end up with a big headache. You would too. Who wants that?

No, Mrs. Jones, we want to handle this problem fairly on the basis of some independent standard, rather than who can do what to whom.

Analysis. Mrs. Jones challenges the idea of negotiating on the basis of principle, calling it a charade. It's a matter of will and her will is to throw out Turnbull and his roommate today.

At this Turnbull almost loses his temper—and with it his control over the negotiation. He feels like counterattacking: "I'd like to see you try to get us out. We'll go to court. We'll get your license revoked." The negotiation would then break off, and Turnbull would lose a lot of time, effort, and peace of mind. But instead of reacting, Turnbull keeps his temper and brings the negotiation back to the merits. This is a good example of negotiation jujitsu. He deflects Mrs. Jones's attack by taking responsibility for her mistaken perceptions, and he tries to persuade her of his sincere interest in principle. He does not hide either his selfish interests or his leverage over her; on the contrary, he makes both explicit. Once they are acknowledged, he can distinguish them from the merits and they can cease being an issue.

Turnbull also tries to give the game of principled negotiation some weight by telling Mrs. Jones this is his basic code — the way he always plays. He attributes this not to high-minded motives — which are always suspect — but to simple self-interest.

"Trust is a separate Issue"

Mrs. Jones: You don't trust me? After all I've done for you?

Turnbull: Mrs. Jones, we appreciate all you've done for us. For us, this is not a matter of trust. The issue is the principle: Did we pay more than we should have? What considerations do you think we should take into account in deciding this?

Analysis. Mrs. Jones tries to manipulate Turnbull into a corner. Either he pursues the point and looks untrusting, or he looks trusting and gives in. Turnbull slips out of the corner, however, by expressing his gratitude once more and then defining the question of trust as irrelevant. Turnbull at once reaffirms his appreciation of Mrs. Jones while he remains firm on the principle. In doing so, he avoids connecting the two thoughts with "but," implicitly using "and" instead. "But," sometimes called the "great eraser," has a tendency to negate the first thing you say by implying that only one of two statements can be true, making it either/or. "And" underscores the more complex reality that both thoughts can be true at the same time. It helps ensure both that Mrs. Jones feels heard and appreciated and that she can't frame Turnbull as wrongly untrusting.

Moreover, instead of just shunting aside the question of trust, Turnbull actively directs the discussion back to principle by asking Mrs. Jones what considerations she thinks are relevant.

Turnbull sticks to principle without blaming Mrs. Jones. He never calls her dishonest. He does not ask, "Did you take advantage of us?" but inquires more impersonally, "Did we pay more than we should have?" Even if he does not trust her, it would be a poor strategy to tell her so. She would probably become defensive and angry and might either withdraw into a rigid position or break off the negotiation altogether.

It helps to have stock phrases like "It's not a question of trust" to turn aside ploys like Mrs. Jones's plea for trust.

"Could I ask you a few questions to see whether my facts are right?"

Turnbull: Could I ask you a few questions to see whether the facts I've been given are right?

Is the apartment really under rent control?

Is the legal maximum rent really $932?

Paul asked me whether this makes us parties to a violation of the law.

Did someone inform Paul at the time he signed the lease that the apartment was under rent control, and that the legal maximum was $268 lower than the rent he agreed to?

Analysis. Statements of fact can feel lecturing or threatening. Whenever you can, ask a question instead.

Turnbull might have declared, "The legal rent is $932. You broke the law. What's worse, you involved us in breaking the law without telling us so." Mrs. Jones would probably have reacted strongly to these statements, dismissing them as verbal attacks intended to score points.

Phrasing each piece of information as a question allows Mrs. Jones to participate, listen to the information, evaluate it, and either accept or correct it. Turnbull communicates the same information to her but in a less provocative manner. He reduces the heat still further by attributing a particularly pointed question to his absent roommate.

In effect, Turnbull induces Mrs. Jones to help lay a foundation of agreed-upon facts upon which a principled solution can be built.

"What's the principle behind your action?"

Turnbull: I'm not clear why you charged us $1,200 a month. What were your reasons for charging that much?

Analysis. A principled negotiator neither accepts nor rejects the other side's positions. To keep the dialogue focused on the merits, Turnbull questions Mrs. Jones about the reasons for her position. He does not ask whether there were any reasons. He assumes there are good reasons. This flattering assumption leads the other side to search for reasons even if there are none, thus keeping the negotiation on the basis of principle.

"Let me see if I understand what you're saying"

Turnbull: Let me see if I understand what you're saying, Mrs. Jones. If I've understood you correctly, you think the rent we paid is fair because you made a lot of repairs and improvements to the apartment since the last rent control evaluation. It wasn't worth your while to ask the Rent Control Board for an increase for the few months you rented the place to us.

In fact, you rented it only as a favor to Paul. And now you're concerned that we may take unfair advantage of you and try to get money from you as the price for moving out. Is there something I've missed or misunderstood?

Analysis. Principled negotiation requires good communication. Before responding to Mrs. Jones's arguments, Turnbull restates to her in positive terms what he has heard to make sure he has indeed understood her.

Once she feels understood, she can relax and discuss the problem constructively. She can't dismiss his arguments on the grounds that they do not take into account what she knows. She is more likely to listen now and be more receptive. In trying to sum up her point of view, Turnbull establishes a cooperative game in which both are making sure he understands the facts.

"Let me get back to you"

Turnbull: Now that I think I understand your point of view, let me talk with my roommate and explain it to him. Can I get back to you tomorrow sometime?

Analysis. A good negotiator rarely makes an important decision on the spot. The psychological pressure to be nice and to give in is too great. A little time and distance help disentangle the people from the problem.

A good negotiator comes to the table with a credible reason in his pocket for leaving when he wants. Such a reason should not indicate passivity or inability to make a decision. Here, Turnbull sounds as if he knows exactly what he is doing, and he arranges to resume the negotiation at a given time. He shows not only decisiveness but also control over the course of the negotiation.

Once away from the table, Turnbull can check on points of information and consult his "constituency," Paul. He can think about the decision and make sure he has not lost perspective.

Too much time at the table may wear down one's commitment to principled negotiation. Returning to the table with renewed resolve, Turnbull can be soft on the person without being soft on the problem.

"Let me show you where I have trouble following some of your reasoning"

Turnbull: Let me show you where I have trouble following some of your reasons for the extra $268 a month. One reason was the repairs and improvements on the apartment. The Rent Control Examiner said it would take about $30,000 in improvements to justify an increase of $268 a month. How much money was spent on improvements?

I must admit it didn't seem like $30,000 worth to Paul and me. The hole in the linoleum you promised to repair was never fixed, neither was the hole in the living room floor. The toilet broke down repeatedly. These are just some of the defects and malfunctions we experienced.

Analysis. In principled negotiation you present your reasons first before offering a proposal. If principles come afterward, they appear not as the objective criteria that any proposal should satisfy but as mere justifications for an arbitrary position.

For Turnbull to explain his reasons first shows his openness to persuasion and his awareness of the need to convince Mrs. Jones. If he announced his proposal first, Mrs. Jones probably would not bother to listen to the reasons that followed. Her mind would be elsewhere, considering what objections and counterproposals she could make.

Turnbull has also sought out objective standards to support his concerns. He has called the Rent Control Board to quantify a correlation between improvements and a $268 per month rent increase. In preparing for your negotiation, it helps to think about what standards would be useful, who might be able to provide them, and how to frame your questions to elicit the most relevant information.

"One fair solution might be . . ."

Turnbull: Given all the considerations we've discussed, one fair solution seems to be for Paul and me to be reimbursed for the amount of rent we paid in excess of the legal maximum. Does that sound fair to you?

Analysis. Turnbull presents a proposal not as *his*, but as a fair option that deserves their joint consideration. He does not claim it is the only fair solution, but *one* fair solution. He is specific without digging himself into a position and inviting rejection.

"If we agree . . . if we disagree . . . "

Turnbull: If you and I could reach agreement now, Paul and I would move out immediately. If we can't reach an agreement, the hearing examiner at the Rent Control Board suggested that we stay in the apartment and withhold rent and/or sue you for reimbursement, treble damages, and legal fees. Paul and I are extremely reluctant to take either of these courses. We feel confident we can settle this matter fairly with you to your satisfaction and ours.

Analysis. Turnbull is trying to make it easy for Mrs. Jones to say yes to his proposal. So he starts by making it clear that all it takes for the problem to go away is Mrs. Jones's agreement.

The trickiest part of the message to communicate is the alternative if no agreement is reached. How can Turnbull get this across—he wants her to take it into account in her decision—without upsetting the negotiations? He bases the alternative on objective principle by attributing it to a legal authority—the hearing examiner. He distances himself personally from the suggestion. Nor does he say he will definitely take action. Instead, he leaves it as a possibility and emphasizes his reluctance to do anything drastic. Finally, he closes by affirming his confidence that a mutually satisfactory agreement will be reached.

Turnbull's BATNA—his best alternative to a negotiated agreement—is probably neither staying in the apartment nor going to court. He and Paul have already rented another apartment and would greatly prefer to move out now. A lawsuit would be difficult, given their busy schedules, and even if they won, they might never be able to collect. Turnbull's BATNA is probably just to move out and stop worrying about the $1,340 overpayment. Since his BATNA is probably less attractive than Mrs. Jones thinks, Turnbull does not disclose it.

"We'd be happy to see if we can leave when it's most convenient for you"

Mrs. Jones: When do you plan to move out?

Turnbull: As long as we've agreed on the appropriate rent for our time in the apartment, we'd be happy to see if we can leave when it's most convenient for you. When would you prefer?

Analysis. Sensing the possibility of a joint gain, Turnbull indicates his willingness to discuss ways of meeting Mrs. Jones's interest. As it turns out, Turnbull and Mrs. Jones have a shared interest in Turnbull moving out as soon as possible.

Incorporating her interests into the agreement not only gives her more of a stake in it but also allows Mrs. Jones to save face. On the one hand, she can feel good about agreeing to a fair solution even though it costs her money. On the other, she can say that she got the tenants out of the apartment early.

"It's been a pleasure dealing with you"

Turnbull: Paul and I do appreciate, Mrs. Jones, all that you've done for us, and I'm pleased that we've settled this last problem fairly and amicably.

Mrs. Jones: Thank you, Mr. Turnbull. Have a nice summer.

Analysis. Turnbull ends the negotiation on a final conciliatory note toward Mrs. Jones. Because they successfully dealt with the problem independently of the relationship, neither party feels cheated or angry, and neither is likely to try to sabotage or ignore their agreement. A working relationship is maintained for the future.

Whether you use principled negotiation and negotiation jujitsu, as Frank Turnbull did, or a third party with the one-text procedure, the conclusion remains the same: you *can* usually get the other side to play the game of principled negotiation with you, even if at first they appear unwilling.

8 What If They Use Dirty Tricks?

(Taming the Hard Bargainer)

Principled negotiation is all very well, but what if the other negotiator deceives you or tries to throw you off balance? Or what if they escalate their demands just when you are on the verge of agreement?

There are many tactics and tricks people can use to try to take advantage of you. Everyone knows some of them. They range from lies and psychological abuse to various forms of pressure tactics. They may be illegal, unethical, or simply unpleasant. Their purpose is to help the user "win" some substantive gain in an unprincipled contest of will. Such tactics may be called tricky bargaining.

If they recognize that a tricky bargaining tactic is being used against them, most people respond in one of two ways. The first standard response is to put up with it. It is unpleasant to rock the boat. You may give the other side the benefit of the doubt or get angry and promise yourself never to deal with them again. For now, you hope for the best and keep quiet. Most people respond this way. They hope that if they give in this time, the other side will be appeased and will not ask for more. Sometimes this works, more often it fails. This is how Neville Chamberlain, the British Prime Minister, responded in 1938 to Hitler's negotiating tactics. After Chamberlain thought he had an agreement, Hitler raised his demands. At Munich, Chamberlain, hoping to avoid war, went along. A year later, World War II started.

The second common response is to respond in kind. If they

start outrageously high, you start outrageously low. If they are deceptive, so are you. If they make threats, you make counter-threats. If they lock themselves into their position, you lock yourself even more tightly into yours. In the end either one party yields or, all too often, negotiation breaks off.

Such tricky tactics are illegitimate because they fail the test of reciprocity. They are designed to be used by only one side; the other side is not supposed to know the tactics or is expected to tolerate them knowingly. Earlier we argued that an effective counter to a one-sided substantive proposal is to examine the legitimacy of the principle that the proposal reflects. Tricky bargaining tactics are in effect one-sided proposals about negotiating *procedure,* about the negotiating game that the parties are going to play. To counter them, you will want to engage in principled negotiation about the negotiating process.

How do you negotiate about the rules of the game?

There are three steps in negotiating the rules of the negotiating game where the other side seems to be using a tricky tactic: recognize the tactic, raise the issue explicitly, and question the tactic's legitimacy and desirability—negotiate over it.

You have to know what is going on to be able to do something about it. Learn to spot particular ploys that indicate deception, those designed to make you uncomfortable, and those that lock the other side into their position. Often just recognizing a tactic will neutralize it. Realizing, for example, that the other side is attacking you personally to impair your judgment may well frustrate the effort.

After recognizing the tactic, consider bringing it up with the other side. "Say, Joe, I may be totally mistaken, but I'm getting the feeling that you and Ted here are playing a good-guy/bad-guy routine. If you two want a recess any time to straighten out differences between you, just ask." Discussing the tactic not only makes it less effective, it also may cause the other side to worry about alienating you completely. Simply raising a question about a tactic may be enough to get them to stop using it.

The most important purpose of bringing the tactic up explicitly, however, is to give you an opportunity to negotiate about the rules of the game. This is the third step. This negotiation focuses on procedure instead of substance, but the goal remains to produce a wise agreement (this time about procedure) efficiently and amicably. Not surprisingly, the method remains the same.

Separate the people from the problem. Don't attack people personally for using a tactic you consider illegitimate. If they get defensive it may be more difficult for them to give up the tactic, and they may be left with a residue of anger that will fester and interfere with other issues. Question the tactic, not their personal integrity. Rather than saying, "You deliberately put me here facing the sun," attack the problem: "I am finding the sun in my eyes quite distracting. Unless we can solve the problem, I may have to leave early to get some rest. Shall we revise the schedule?" It will be easier to reform the negotiating process than to reform those with whom you are dealing. Don't be diverted from the negotiation by the urge to teach them a lesson.

Focus on interests, not positions. "Why are you committing yourself in the press to an extreme position? Are you trying to protect yourself from criticism? Or are you protecting yourself from changing your position? Is it in our mutual interest to have both of us use this tactic?"

Invent options for mutual gain. Suggest alternative games to play. "How about our undertaking to make no statements to the press until we reach agreement or break off the talks?"

Insist on using objective criteria. Above all, be hard on principle. "Is there a theory behind having me sit in the low chair with my back to the open door?" Try out the principle of reciprocity on them. "I assume that you will sit in this chair tomorrow morning?" Frame the principle behind each tactic as a proposed "rule" for the game. "Shall we alternate spilling coffee on one another day by day?"

As a last resort, turn to your BATNA (your Best Alternative To a Negotiated Agreement) and walk out. "It's my impression that you're not interested in negotiating in a way that we both think will produce results. Here's my phone number. If I'm mistaken, I'm ready any time you are. Until then, we'll pursue the court option." If you are walking out on clearly legitimate grounds, as when they have deliberately deceived you about facts or their authority, and if they are genuinely interested in an agreement, they are likely to call you back to the table.

Some common tricky tactics

Tricky tactics can be divided into three categories: deliberate deception, psychological warfare, and positional pressure tactics. You should be prepared to deal with all three. Below are a number of common examples of each type; for each in turn, we show how principled negotiation might be applied to counter it.

Deliberate deception

Perhaps the most common form of dirty trick is misrepresentation about facts, authority, or intentions.

Phony facts. The oldest form of negotiating trickery is to make some knowingly false statement: "This car was driven only 5,000 miles by a little old lady from Pasadena who never went over 35 miles per hour." The dangers of being taken in by false statements are great. What can you do?

Disentangle the people from the problem. Unless you have good reason to trust somebody, don't. This does not mean calling him a liar; rather it means making the negotiation proceed independent of trust. Do not let someone treat your doubts as a personal attack. No seller is likely to give you a watch or a car simply in exchange for your statement that you have money in the bank. Just as a seller will routinely check on your credit ("because there are so many other people around that can't be trusted"), you can do the same for statements of the other side. A practice of verifying factual assertions reduces the incentive for deception, and your risk of being cheated.

Ambiguous authority. The other side may allow you to believe that they, like you, have full authority to compromise when they don't. After they have pressed you as hard as they can and you have worked out what you believe to be a firm agreement, they announce that they must take it to someone else for approval. This technique is designed to give them a "second bite at the apple."

This is a bad situation to fall into. If only *you* have authority to make concessions, only you will make concessions.

Do not assume that the other side has full authority just because they are there negotiating with you. An insurance adjuster, a lawyer, or a salesperson may allow you to think that your flexibility is being matched by flexibility on their side. You may later find that what you thought was an agreement will be treated by the other side as simply a floor for further negotiation.

Before starting on any give-and-take, find out about the authority on the other side. It is perfectly legitimate to inquire, "Just how much authority do you have in this particular negotiation?" If the answer is ambiguous, you may wish to talk to someone with real authority or to make clear that you on your side are reserving equal freedom to reconsider any point.

If they do announce unexpectedly that they are treating what you thought was an agreement as a basis for further negotiation, insist on reciprocity. "All right. We will treat it as a joint draft to which neither side is committed. You check with your boss and I'll sleep on it and see if I come up with any changes I want to suggest tomorrow." Or you might say, "If your boss approves this draft tomorrow, I'll stick by it. Otherwise each of us should feel free to propose changes."

One way to try to head off this problem is to clarify early in the negotiation that "nothing is agreed until everything is agreed," so that any effort to reopen one issue automatically reopens all issues.

Dubious intentions. Where the issue is one of possible misrepresentation of their intention to comply with the agreement, it is often possible to build compliance features into the agreement itself.

Suppose you are a lawyer representing the wife in a divorce negotiation. Your client does not believe her husband will pay child support even though he may agree to do so. The time and energy spent in going to court every month may lead her to give up the effort. What can you do? Make the problem explicit and use their protestations to get a guarantee. You could say to the husband's lawyer, "Look, my client is afraid those child support payments simply aren't going to be made. Rather than monthly payments, how about giving her equity in the house?" The husband's lawyer may say, "My client is perfectly trustworthy. We'll put it in writing that he will pay child support regularly." To which you might respond, "It's not a matter of trust. Are you certain that your client will pay?"

"Of course."

"A hundred percent certain?"

"Yes, I'm a hundred percent certain."

"Then you won't mind a contingent agreement. Your client will agree to make child support payments. We'll provide that if, for some inexplicable reason that you estimate at zero percent probability, he misses two payments, my client will get the equity in the house (minus, of course, the amount your client has already paid out in child support) and your client will no longer be liable for child support." It is not easy for the husband's lawyer to object.

Less than full disclosure is not the same as deception. Deliberate deception as to facts or one's intentions is quite different from not fully disclosing one's present thinking. Good faith negotiation does not require total disclosure. Perhaps the best answer to questions such as "What is the most you would pay if you had to?" would be along the following lines: "Let's not put ourselves under such a strong temptation to mislead. If you think no agreement is possible, and that we may be wasting our time, perhaps we could disclose our thinking to some trustworthy third party, who can then tell us whether there is a zone of potential agreement." In this way it is possible to behave with full candor about information that is not being disclosed.

Psychological warfare

These tactics are designed to make you feel uncomfortable, so that you will have a subconscious desire to end the negotiation as soon as possible.

Stressful situations. Much has been written about the physical circumstances in which negotiations take place. You should be sensitive to such modest questions as whether a meeting takes place at your place or theirs, or on neutral territory. Contrary to the accepted wisdom, it is sometimes advantageous to accept an offer to meet on the other side's turf. It may put them at ease, making them more open to your suggestions. If necessary, it will be easier for you to walk out. If, however, you do allow the other side to choose the physical environment, be aware of what that choice is and what effects it may have.

Ask yourself if you feel under stress, and if so, why. If the room is too noisy, if the temperature is too hot or cold, if there is no place for a private caucus with a colleague, be aware that the setting might have been deliberately designed to make you want to conclude negotiations promptly and, if necessary, to yield points to do so.

If you find the physical surroundings prejudicial, do not hesitate to say so. You can suggest changing chairs, taking a break, or adjourning to a different location or another time. In every case your job is to identify the problem, be willing to raise it with the other side, and then negotiate better physical circumstances in an objective and principled fashion.

Personal attacks. In addition to manipulating the physical environment, there are also ways for the other side to use verbal and nonverbal communication to make you feel uncomfortable.

They can comment on your clothes or your appearance. "Looks like you were up all night. Things not going well at the office?" They can attack your status by making you wait for them or by interrupting the negotiations to deal with other people. They can imply that you are ignorant. They can refuse to listen to you and make you repeat yourself. They can deliberately refuse to make eye contact with you. (Simple experiments with students have confirmed the malaise many feel when this tactic is used, and they are unable to identify the cause of the problem.) In each case recognizing the tactic will help nullify its effect; bringing it up explicitly will probably prevent a recurrence.

The good-guy/bad-guy routine. One form of psychological pressure that also involves deception is the good-guy/bad-guy routine. This technique appears in its starkest form in old police movies. The first policeman threatens the suspect with prosecution for numerous crimes, puts him under a bright light, pushes him around, then finally takes a break and leaves. The good guy then turns off the light, offers the suspect a cigarette, and apologizes for the tough policeman. He says he'd like to control the tough guy, but he can't unless the suspect cooperates. The result: the suspect tells all he knows.

Similarly in a negotiation, two people on the same side will stage a quarrel. One will take a tough stand: "This business is worth $80,000 and I won't accept a penny less." His partner looks pained and a little embarrassed. Finally he breaks in: "Frank, you are being unreasonable. After all, cash flow is a little down, even if receivables are strong." Turning to the other side, he says reasonably, "Could you pay $76,000?" The concession isn't large, but it almost seems like a favor.

The good-guy/bad-guy routine is a form of psychological manipulation. If you recognize it, you won't be taken in. When the good guy makes his pitch, just ask him the same question you asked the bad guy: "I appreciate that you are trying to be reasonable, and I still want to know why you think that's a fair price. What is your principle? I am prepared to pay $80,000 if you can persuade me it's the fairest price."

Threats. Threats are one of the most abused tactics in negotiation. A threat seems easy to make — much easier than an offer. All it takes is a few words, and if it works, you never have to carry it out. But threats can lead to counterthreats in an escalating spiral that can unhinge a negotiation and even destroy a relationship.

Threats are pressure. Pressure often accomplishes just the opposite of what it is intended to do; it builds up pressure the other way. Instead of making a decision easier for the other side, it often makes it more difficult. In response to outside pressure, a union, a committee, a company, or a government may close ranks. Moderates and hawks join together to resist what they may perceive as an illegitimate attempt to coerce them. The question changes from "Should we make this decision?" to "Shall we cave in to outside pressure?"

Good negotiators rarely resort to threats. They do not need to; there are other ways to communicate the same information. If it seems appropriate to outline the consequences of the other side's action, suggest those that will occur independently of your will rather than those you could choose to bring about. *Warnings* are much more legitimate than threats and are not vulnerable to counterthreats: "Should we fail to reach agreement, it seems highly probable to me that the news media would insist on publishing the whole sordid story. In a matter of this much public interest, I don't see how we could legitimately or realistically suppress information. Do you?"

You can also warn the other side about your likely actions in the event of no agreement, so long as you can show how those actions are intended to safeguard your interests, *not* to coerce or punish the other side. "So you are not surprised, here is a draft of the press release we plan to issue if our contract is not renewed." If the other side finds this prospect unpleasant, they may react by asking, "Are you threatening me?" Provided your plans are a true warning, you should be able to reply confidently, "Absolutely not. In our shoes, would you recommend a better way to safeguard our interests?"

For threats to be effective they must be credibly communicated. Sometimes you can interfere with the communication process. You can ignore threats; you can take them as unauthorized, spoken in haste, or simply irrelevant. You can also make it risky to communicate them. At a coal mine where one of the authors was recently mediating, a large number of false but costly bomb threats were being received. These dropped off dramatically when the company's receptionist began answering all phone calls with "Your voice is being recorded. What number are you calling?"

Sometimes threats can be turned to your political advantage. A union could announce to the press: "Management has such a weak case that they are resorting to threats." Perhaps the best response to a threat, however, is to be principled. "We have prepared a sequence of countermoves for each of management's customary threats. However, we have delayed taking action until we see whether we can agree that making threats is not the most constructive activity we could engage in just now." Or "I only negotiate on the merits. My reputation is built on not responding to threats."

Positional pressure tactics

This kind of bargaining tactic is designed to structure the situation so that only one side can effectively make concessions.

Refusal to negotiate. When the American diplomats and embassy personnel were taken hostage in Tehran in November 1979, the Iranian government announced its demands and refused to negotiate. A lawyer will often do the same, simply telling opposing counsel, "I'll see you in court." What can you do when the other side refuses to negotiate altogether?

First, recognize the tactic as a possible negotiating ploy: an attempt to use their entry into negotiation as a bargaining chip to obtain some concession on substance. A variant on this ploy is to set preconditions for negotiations.

Second, talk about their refusal to negotiate. Communicate either directly or through third parties. Don't attack them for refusing to negotiate, but rather find out their interests in not negotiating. Are they worried about giving you status by talking to you? Will those who talk with you be criticized for being "soft"? Do they think negotiation will destroy their precarious internal unity? Or do they simply not believe that an agreement is possible?

Suggest some options, such as negotiating through third parties, sending letters, or encouraging private individuals like journalists to discuss the issues (as happened in the Iranian case).

Finally, insist on using principles. Is this the way they would want you to play? Do they want you to set preconditions as well? Will they want others to refuse to negotiate with them? What are the principles they think should apply to this situation?

Extreme demands. Negotiators will frequently start with extreme proposals like offering $175,000 for your house that is apparently worth $300,000. The goal is to lower your expectations. They also figure that an extreme initial position will give them a better end result, on the theory that the parties will ultimately end up splitting the difference between their positions. There are drawbacks to this approach, even for tricky bargainers. Making an extreme demand that both you and they know will be abandoned undermines their credibility. Such an opening may also kill the deal; if they offer too little, you may think they are not worth bothering with.

Bringing the tactic to their attention works well here. Ask for principled justification of their position until it looks ridiculous even to them.

Escalating demands. A negotiator may raise one of his demands for every concession he makes on another. He may also reopen issues you thought had been settled. The benefits of this tactic lie in decreasing the overall concession, and in the psychological effect of making you want to agree quickly before he raises any more of his demands.

The Prime Minister of Malta used this tactic in negotiating with Great Britain in 1971 over the price of naval and air base rights. Each time the British thought they had an agreement, he would say, "Yes, agreed, but there is still one small problem." And the small problem would turn out to be a £10 million cash advance or guaranteed jobs for dockyard and base workers for the life of the contract.

When you recognize this, call it to their attention and then perhaps take a break while you consider whether and on what basis you want to continue negotiations. This avoids an impulsive reaction while indicating the seriousness of their conduct. And again, insist on principle. When you come back, anyone interested in settlement will be more serious.

Lock-in tactics. This tactic is illustrated by Thomas Schelling's well-known example of two dynamite trucks barreling toward each other on a single-lane road. The question becomes which truck goes off the road to avoid an accident. As the trucks near each other, one driver in full view of the other pulls off his steering wheel and throws it out the window. Seeing this, the other driver has a choice between an explosive crash or driving his truck off the road into a ditch. This is an example of an extreme commitment tactic designed to make it impossible to yield. Paradoxically, you strengthen your bargaining position by weakening your control over the situation.

In labor-management and international negotiations this tactic is common. A union president makes a rousing speech to her constituency pledging that she will never accept less than a 15 percent salary increase. Since she stands to lose face and credibility if she does agree to anything less, she can more convincingly persuade management the union must have 15 percent.

But lock-in tactics are gambles. You may call the other side's bluff and force them to make a concession, which they will then have to explain to their constituency.

Like threats, lock-in tactics depend on communication. If the other truck driver does not see the steering wheel fly out the window, or if he thinks the truck has an emergency steering mechanism, the act of throwing the steering wheel out the window will not have its intended effect. The pressure to avoid a collision will be felt equally by both drivers.

In response to a commitment tactic, therefore, you may be able to interrupt the communication. You can so interpret the commitment as to weaken it. "Oh, I see. You told the papers your *goal* was to settle for $400,000. Well, we all have our aspirations, I guess. Do you want to know what mine are?" Alternatively, you can crack a joke and not take the lock-in seriously.

You can also resist lock-ins on principle: "Fine, Bob, I understand you made that statement publicly. But my practice is never to yield to pressure, only to reason. Now let's talk about the merits of the problem." Whatever you do, avoid making the commitment a central question. Deemphasize it so that the other side can more gracefully back down.

Hardhearted partner. Perhaps the most common negotiating tactic used to justify not yielding to your requests is for the other negotiator to say that he personally would have no objection, but his hardhearted partner will not let him. "It's a perfectly reasonable request, I agree. But my boss absolutely refuses to hear of it."

Recognize the tactic. Rather than discussing it with the other negotiator, you may want to get his agreement to the principle involved—perhaps in writing—and then if possible speak directly with the "hardhearted partner."

A calculated delay. Frequently one side will try to postpone coming to a decision until a time they think favorable. Labor negotiators will often delay until the last few hours before a strike deadline, relying on the psychological pressure of the deadline to make management more malleable. Unfortunately, they often miscalculate and the strike deadline passes. Once the strike begins, management, in turn, may decide to wait for a more favorable time, such as when the union's strike fund has run out. Waiting for the right time is a high-cost game.

In addition to making delaying tactics explicit and negotiating about them, consider creating a fading opportunity for the other side. If you represent one company negotiating a merger with another, start talks with a third company, exploring the possibility of merging with them instead. Look for objective conditions that can be used to establish credible deadlines, such as the date on which taxes are due, the annual trustees meeting, the end of the contract, or the end of the legislative session.

"Take it or leave it." There is nothing inherently wrong with confronting the other side with a firm choice. In fact, most American business is conducted this way. If you go into a supermarket and see a can of beans marked $1.50, you don't normally try to negotiate with the supermarket manager. This is an efficient method of conducting business, but it is not negotiation. It is not interactive decision-making. Nor is there anything wrong after long negotiations to conclude them when you mean to do so by saying, "Take it or leave it," except that you should probably phrase it more politely.

As an alternative to explicitly recognizing the "Take it or leave it" tactic and negotiating about it, consider ignoring it at first. Keep talking as if you didn't hear it, or change the subject, perhaps by introducing other solutions. If you do bring up the tactic specifically, let them know what they have to lose if no agreement is reached and look for a face-saving way, such as a change in circumstances, for them to get out of the situation. After management has announced its final offer, the union could tell them, "A $3.69 per hour raise was your final offer before we discussed our cooperative efforts to make the plant more productive."

Don't be a victim

It is often hard to decide what it means to negotiate in "good faith." People draw the line in different places. It may help to ask yourself such questions as: Is this an approach I would use in dealing with a good friend or a member of my family? If a full account of what I said and did appeared in the media, would I be embarrassed? In literature, would such conduct be more appropriate for a hero or a villain? These questions are not intended to bring external opinion to bear so much as to shed light on your own internal values. You must decide on your own whether you want to use tactics you would consider improper and in bad faith if used against you.

It may be useful at the beginning of the negotiation to say, "Look, I know this may be unusual, but I want to know the rules of the game we're going to play. Are we both trying to reach a wise agreement as quickly and with as little effort as possible? Or are we going to play 'hard bargaining' where the more stubborn fellow wins?" Whatever you do, be prepared to fight tricky bargaining tactics. You can be just as firm as they can, even firmer. It is easier to defend principle than an illegitimate tactic. Don't be a victim.

IV IN CONCLUSION

In Conclusion

Three points.

You knew it all the time

There is probably nothing in this book that you did not already know at some level of your experience. What we have tried to do is to organize common sense and common experience in a way that provides a usable framework for thinking and acting. The more consistent these ideas are with your knowledge and intuition the better. In teaching this method to skilled lawyers and businesspeople with years of experience, we have been told, "Now I know what I have been doing, and why it sometimes works" and "I knew what you were saying was right because I knew it already."

Learn from doing

A book can point you in a promising direction. By making you aware of ideas and aware of what you are doing, it can help you learn.

No one, however, can make you skillful but yourself. Reading a pamphlet on the Royal Canadian Air Force fitness program will not make you physically fit. Studying books on tennis, swimming, riding a bicycle, or riding a horse will not make you an expert. Negotiation is no different.

"Winning"

In 1964 an American father and his twelve-year-old son were enjoying a beautiful Saturday in Hyde Park, London, playing catch with a Frisbee. Few in England had seen a Frisbee at that time and a small group of strollers gathered to watch this strange sport. Finally, one homburg-clad Englishman came over to the father: "Sorry to bother you. Been watching you a quarter of an hour. Who's *winning?*"

In most instances to ask a negotiator "Who's winning?" is as inappropriate as to ask who's winning a marriage. If you ask that question about your marriage, you have already lost the more important negotiation—the one about what kind of game to play, about the way you deal with each other and your shared and differing interests.

This book is about how to "win" that important game—how to achieve a better process for dealing with your differences. To be better, the process must, of course, produce good substantive results; winning on the merits may not be the only goal, but certainly losing is not the answer. Both theory and experience suggest that the method of principled negotiation will produce over the long run substantive outcomes as good as or better than you are likely to obtain using any other negotiation strategy. In addition, it should prove more efficient and less costly to human relationships. We find the method comfortable to use and hope you will too.

That does not mean it is easy to change habits, to disentangle emotions from the merits, or to enlist others in the task of working out a wise solution to a shared problem. From time to time you may want to remind yourself that the first thing you are trying to win is a better way to negotiate—a way that avoids your having to choose between the satisfactions of getting what you deserve and of being decent. You can have both.

V TEN QUESTIONS PEOPLE ASK ABOUT *GETTING TO YES*

Questions About Fairness and "Principled" Negotiation
1. "Does positional bargaining *ever* make sense?"
2. "What if the other side believes in a different standard of fairness?"
3. "Should I be fair if I don't have to be?"

Questions About Dealing with People
4. "What do I do if the people *are* the problem?"
5. "Should I negotiate even with terrorists or someone like Hitler? When does it make sense *not* to negotiate?"
6. "How should I adjust my negotiating approach to account for differences of personality, gender, culture, and so on?"

Questions About Tactics
7. "How do I decide things like 'Where should we meet?' 'How should we communicate?' 'Who should make the first offer?' and 'How high should I start?'"
8. "Concretely, how do I move from inventing options to making commitments?"
9. "How do I try out these ideas without taking too much risk?"

Questions About Power
10. "Can the way I negotiate really make a difference if the other side is more powerful?" And "How do I enhance *my* negotiating power?"

Ten Questions People Ask About *Getting to YES*

QUESTIONS ABOUT FAIRNESS AND "PRINCIPLED" NEGOTIATION

Question 1: "Does positional bargaining *ever* make sense?"

Positional bargaining is easy, so it is not surprising that people often do it. It requires no preparation, it is universally understood (sometimes you can even do it with fingers when you and the other side do not share a common language), and in some contexts it is entrenched and expected. In contrast, looking behind positions for interests, inventing options for mutual gain, and finding and using objective criteria take hard work and, when the other side seems recalcitrant, emotional restraint and maturity.

In virtually every case, the outcome will be better for both sides with principled negotiation. The issue is whether it is worth the extra effort. Here are some questions to consider:

How important is it to avoid an arbitrary outcome? If, like the house builder in Chapter 5, you are negotiating over how deep to build your home's foundations, you will not want to haggle over arbitrary positions no matter how much easier it might be to reach agreement. Even if you are negotiating for a one-of-a-kind antique chamber pot, where objective standards will be hard to find, exploring the dealer's interests and looking for creative options is probably a good idea. Still, one factor to consider in choosing a negotiating approach is how much you care about finding an answer to the problem that makes sense on the merits. The stakes would be much higher if you were negotiating over the foundations for an office building than those for a tool shed. They will also be higher if this transaction will set a precedent for future transactions.

How complex are the issues? The more complex the subject matter, the more unwise it is to engage in positional bargaining. Complexity calls for careful analysis of interests that are shared or that can be creatively dovetailed, and then for brainstorming. Both will be easier to the extent the parties see themselves as engaged in joint problem-solving.

How important is it to maintain a good working relationship? If the other side is a valued customer or client, maintaining your ongoing relationship may be more important to you than the outcome of any one deal. This does not mean you should be less persistent in pursuing your interests, but it does suggest avoiding tactics such as threats or ultimatums that involve a high risk of damage to the relationship. Negotiation on the merits helps avoid a choice between giving in or angering the other side.

In single-issue negotiations among strangers where the transaction costs of exploring interests would be high and where each side is protected by competitive opportunities, simple haggling over positions may work fine. But if the discussion starts to bog down, be prepared to change gears. Start clarifying the underlying interests.

You should also consider the effect of this negotiation on your relationship with others. Is this negotiation likely to affect your reputation as a negotiator and, consequently, how others approach negotiating with you? If so, what effect would you like it to have?

What are the other side's expectations, and how hard would they be to change? In many labor-management and other contexts, the parties have a long history of hard-fought and almost ritualistic positional bargaining. Each side sees the other as "the enemy" and the situation as zero-sum, ignoring the enormous shared costs of strikes, lockouts, and bad feelings. In these situations it is not easy to establish joint problem-solving, yet it may be correspondingly more important. Even parties that would like to change often find it hard in practice to shed old habits: to listen instead of attacking, to brainstorm instead of quarreling, and to explore interests before making a commitment. Some parties locked into adversarial ruts seem unable to consider alternative approaches until they reach the brink of mutual annihilation, and some not even then. In such contexts you will want to set a realistic timetable for change that may span several complete negotiations. It took General Motors and the United Auto Workers four contracts to change the fundamental structure of their negotiations, and there remain constituents on each side who are not yet comfortable with the new regime.

Where are you in the negotiation? Bargaining over positions tends to inhibit looking for joint gains. In many negotiations, the parties end up with outcomes that "leave a lot of gold on the table." Bargaining over positions does the least harm if it comes *after* you have identified each other's interests, invented options for mutual gain, and discussed relevant standards of fairness.

Question 2: "What if the other side believes in a different standard of fairness?"

In most negotiations there will be no one "right" or "fairest" answer; people will advance different standards by which to judge what is fair. Yet using external standards improves on haggling in three ways: An outcome informed even by conflicting standards of fairness and community practice is likely to be wiser than an arbitrary result. Using standards reduces the costs of "backing down"—it is easier to agree to follow a principle or independent standard than to give in to the other side's positional demand. And finally, unlike arbitrary positions, some standards are more persuasive than others.

In a negotiation between a young lawyer and a Wall Street law firm over salary, for example, it would be absurd for the hiring partner to say, "I don't suppose you think you are any smarter than I am, so we'll offer you the same salary I made when I started out forty years ago—$24,000." The young lawyer would point out the impact of inflation over the intervening years and suggest using current salaries. If the partner proposed using the current salaries for young lawyers in Dayton or Des Moines, the young lawyer would point out that the average salary for young lawyers in similarly prestigious Manhattan firms was a more appropriate standard.

Explore how conflicting standards have developed. Usually one standard will be more persuasive than another to the extent that it is more directly on point, more widely accepted, and more immediately relevant in terms of time, place, and circumstance. When that isn't obvious, it is helpful to ask why and how conflicting standards have developed. Is the market in transition, for example, in the midst of evolving to a new structure with different expectations and standards? Or are two traditions converging? By understanding the logic and history of how standards have developed, you can better argue which are more appropriate in your situation. In many industries, for example, the advent of the Internet has undercut the traditional role of local distributors, with many buyers wanting to buy online or direct from manufacturers. Traditional standards of a reasonable distributor profit margin are in sharp conflict with competitive market prices, leading to new conversations about the value of service and local access. Over time, distributors evolve their business models or go out of business.

Agreement on the "best" standard is not necessary. Differences in values, culture, experience, and perceptions may well lead parties to disagree about the relative merits of different standards. If it were necessary to agree on which standard was "best," settling a negotiation might not be possible. But agreement on criteria is not necessary. Criteria are just one tool that may help the parties find an agreement better for both than no agreement. Using external standards often helps narrow the range of disagreement and may help expand the area of potential agreement. When standards have been refined to the point that it is difficult to argue persuasively that one standard is more applicable than another, the parties can explore trade-offs or resort to fair procedures to settle the remaining differences. They can flip a coin, use an arbitrator, or even split the difference.

Question 3: "Should I be fair if I don't have to be?"

Getting to YES is not a sermon on the morality of right and wrong; it is a book on how to do well in a negotiation. We do not suggest that you should be good for the sake of being good (nor do we discourage it).* We do not suggest that you give in to the first offer that is arguably within the realm of fairness. Nor do we suggest that you never ask for more than what a judge or jury might think is fair. We argue only that using independent standards to discuss the fairness of a proposal is an idea that can help you get what you deserve and protect you from getting taken.

If you want more than you can justify as fair and find that you are regularly able to persuade others to give it to you, you may not find some of the suggestions in this book all that useful. But the negotiators we meet more often fear getting *less* than they should in a negotiation, or damaging a relationship if they press firmly for what they do deserve. The ideas in this book are meant to show you how to get what you are entitled to while still getting along with the other side.

Nevertheless, sometimes you may have an opportunity to get more than you think would be fair. Should you take it? In our opinion, not without careful thought. More is at stake than just a choice about your moral self-definition. (That too probably

---

* We do think that, in addition to providing a good all-around method for getting what you want in a negotiation, principled negotiation can help make the world a better place. It promotes understanding among people, whether they be parent and child, worker and manager, or Arab and Israeli. Focusing on interests and creative options helps increase satisfaction and minimize waste. Relying on standards of fairness and seeking to meet the interests of *both* sides helps produce agreements that are durable, set good precedents, and build lasting relationships. The more a problem-solving approach to negotiation becomes the norm in dealing with differences among individuals and nations, the lower will be the costs of conflict. And beyond such social benefits, you may find that using this approach serves values of caring and justice in a way that is personally satisfying.

deserves careful thought, but advising in that realm is not our purpose here.) Presented with the opportunity to get more than you think is fair, you should weigh the possible benefits against the potential costs of accepting the windfall:

How much is the difference worth to you? What is the most that you could justify to yourself as fair? Just how important to you is the excess above that standard? Weigh this benefit against the risk of incurring some of the costs listed below, and then consider whether there might not be better options. (For example, could the proposed transaction be structured so that the other side sees themselves as doing you a favor rather than getting ripped off?)

It would also be wise to consider how certain you are of these potential benefits. Might you be overlooking something? Is the other side really so blind? Many negotiators are overly optimistic in assuming that they are more clever than their counterparts.

Will the unfair result be durable? If the other side later concludes that an agreement is unfair, they may be unwilling to carry it out. What would it cost to try to enforce the agreement or to replace it? Courts may refuse to enforce an agreement found to be "unconscionable."

You should also consider where you are in the negotiation. There is no value in a super-favorable tentative agreement if the other side wakes up and repudiates it before it becomes final. And if the other side concludes from the incident that you are an untrustworthy lout out to take advantage of them, the cost may not be limited to this provision of this agreement.

What damage might the unfair result cause to this or other relationships? How likely is it that you will find yourself negotiating with this same party again? If you did, what might be the risks for you if they were "out for revenge"? How about your reputation with other people, especially your reputation for fair dealing? Might it be adversely affected more than would offset your immediate gain?

A well-established reputation for fair dealing can be an extraordinary asset. It opens up a large realm of creative agreements that would be impossible if others did not trust you. Such a reputation is much easier to destroy than to build.

Will your conscience bother you? Are you likely later to regret the agreement, believing that you took unfair advantage of someone? Consider the tourist who bought a beautiful Kashmir rug from the family who had labored for a full year to make it. He cleverly offered to pay in German currency, then offered worthless bills from the inflationary pre-WWII Weimar period. Only when he told the story to shocked friends back home did he begin to think about what he had done to this family. In time, the very sight of his beautiful rug turned his stomach. Like this tourist, many people find that they care about more in life than money and "beating" the other side.

QUESTIONS ABOUT DEALING WITH PEOPLE

Question 4: "What do I do if the people *are* the problem?"

Some people have interpreted the admonition "Separate the people from the problem" to mean sweep people problems under the rug. This is emphatically *not* what we mean. People problems often require more attention than substantive ones. The human propensity for defensive and reactive behavior is one reason so many negotiations fail when agreement would otherwise make sense. In negotiation you ignore people issues—how you are treating the other side—at your peril. Our basic advice is the same whether people problems are one concern or the main focus of your negotiation:

Build a working relationship independent of agreement or disagreement. The more seriously you disagree with someone, the more important it is that you be able to deal well with that disagreement. A good working relationship is one that can cope with differences. Such a relationship cannot be bought by making substantive concessions or by pretending that disagreements do not exist. Experience suggests that appeasement does not often work. Making an unjustified concession now is unlikely to make it easier to deal with future differences. You may think that next time it is their turn to make a concession; they are likely to believe that if they are stubborn enough, you will again give in. (Neville Chamberlain's agreement to German occupation of the Sudetenland and the lack of military response to Hitler's subsequent occupation of all of Czechoslovakia probably encouraged the Nazis to believe that an invasion of Poland would also not lead to war.)

Nor should you try to coerce a substantive concession by threatening the relationship. ("If you really cared for me, you would give in." "Unless you agree with me, our relationship is through.") Whether or not such a ploy succeeds for the moment in obtaining a concession, it will damage the relationship. It will tend to make it more difficult for the two sides to deal well with future differences.

Rather, substantive issues need to be *disentangled* from relationship and process issues. The content of a possible agreement needs to be separated from questions of how you talk about it and how you deal with the other side. Each set of issues needs to be negotiated on its own merits. The following list illustrates the distinction:

Substantive Issues
- Terms
- Conditions
- Prices
- Dates
- Numbers
- Liabilities

Relationship Issues
- Balance of emotion and reason
- Ease of communication
- Degree of trust and reliability
- Attitude of acceptance (or rejection)

- Relative emphasis on persuasion (or coercion)
- Degree of mutual understanding

People often assume that there is a trade-off between pursuing a good substantive outcome and pursuing a good relationship. We disagree. A good working relationship tends to make it easier to get good substantive outcomes (for both sides). Good substantive outcomes tend to make a good relationship even better.

Sometimes there may be good reasons to agree, even when you believe fairness would dictate otherwise. For example, if you already have an excellent working relationship, you may well decide to give in on an issue, confident that on some future occasion the other person will recognize that they "owe you one" and reciprocate the favor. (But make sure they also see what you are doing as a favor.) Or you may reasonably decide that one or more issues are not worth fighting over, all things considered. Our point is that you should not give in for the purpose of trying to improve a relationship.

Negotiate the relationship. If, despite your efforts to establish a working relationship and to negotiate substantive differences on their merits, people problems still stand in the way, negotiate them—on *their* merits. Raise your concerns about the other side's behavior and discuss them as you would a substantive difference. Avoid judging them or impugning their motivations. Rather, explain your perceptions and feelings and inquire into theirs. Propose external standards or fair principles to determine how you should deal with each other and decline to give in to pressure tactics. Frame your discussion as looking forward, not back, and operate on the assumptions that the other side may not intend all the consequences you experience and that they can change their approach if they see the need.

As always in negotiation, you need to have thought through your BATNA. In some cases the other side may come to appreciate that your concerns are a *shared* problem only when they realize that your BATNA, in the event you fail to reach a solution satisfactory to you, is not very good for them.

Distinguish how you treat them from how they treat you.
There is no need to emulate unconstructive behavior. Doing so
may indeed "teach them a lesson," though often not the lesson
we would like. In most cases responding in kind reinforces the
behavior we dislike. It encourages the other side to feel that
everyone behaves that way and that it is the only way to protect
themselves. Our behavior should be designed to model and encourage the behavior we would prefer and to avoid any reward
for the behavior we dislike, both without compromising our substantive interests.

Deal rationally with apparent irrationality. Much—perhaps
most—behavior in the world is not very rational. As we say in
Chapter 2, negotiators are people first. We often act impulsively
or react without careful thought, especially when we are angry,
afraid, or frustrated. And we all know people who seem just
plain irrational no matter the situation. How do you cope with
such behavior?

First, recognize that, while people often do not negotiate rationally, it is worth trying to yourself. In a mental hospital, we do not
want psychotic doctors. Likewise, in coping with the irrationality
of other negotiators, you would like to be as purposive as possible.

Second, question your assumption that others are acting irra-
tionally. Perhaps they see the situation differently. In most conflicts, each side believes that they are reasonably saying "no" to
what they hear the other demanding. Perhaps they hear your well-
padded opening position as unjustifiable on the merits; perhaps
they value things differently; or there may be a communication
failure.

Sometimes people do hold views that many of us think are
objectively "irrational," such as people who fear flying. Inter-
nally, however, these people are reacting rationally to the world
as they see it. At some level, they believe that *this* plane will
crash. If we believed that, we would not fly either. It is the perception that is skewed, not the response to that perception. Neither
telling such people that they are wrong (with however many sci-

entific studies) nor punishing them for their beliefs is likely to change how they feel. On the other hand, if you inquire empathetically, taking their feelings seriously and trying to trace their reasoning to its roots, it is sometimes possible to effect change. Working with them, you may discover a logical leap, a factual misperception, or a traumatic association from an earlier time that, once brought to light, can be examined and modified by the people themselves. In essence, you are looking for the psychological interests behind their position, to help them find a way to meet more of their interests more effectively.

Question 5: "Should I negotiate even with terrorists or someone like Hitler? When does it make sense *not* to negotiate?"

However unsavory the other side, unless you have a better BATNA, the question you face is not whether to negotiate, but *how*.

Negotiate with terrorists? Yes. In fact, in the sense that you are trying to influence their decisions—and they are trying to influence yours—you are negotiating with them even if you are not talking with them. The question is whether to do so at a distance by actions and words (such as "We will never negotiate with terrorists!") or whether to do so more directly. In general, the better the communication, the better your chance to exert influence. If questions of personal safety can be resolved, it might make sense to establish a dialogue with terrorists, whether they are holding hostages or threatening some act of violence. If you have a good case, you are more likely to influence them than they are to influence you. (The same arguments apply to dealing with negotiation "terrorists," who try to use dirty tricks.)

Negotiation does not mean giving in. There are high costs in paying ransom or blackmail. Rewarding kidnapping encourages more kidnapping. Through communication it may be possible to convince terrorists (and possible future terrorists) that they will not receive a ransom. It may also be possible to learn of some legitimate interests they have and to work out an arrangement in which neither side gives in.

With the help of Algerian mediators, the United States and Iran were able to negotiate the release in January 1981 of the American diplomats who had been held for more than a year in the U.S. embassy in Tehran. The basis of the settlement was that *each side got no more than that to which they were entitled:* The hostages would be released; Iran would pay its debts; when those amounts were settled, the balance of the funds seized by the United States would be returned to Iran; the United States would recognize the government of Iran and would not interfere in its internal affairs; and so on. It would have been difficult if not impossible to work out a settlement without negotiation. And despite the gross illegality of the seizure of the U.S. embassy, both sides benefited from the negotiations that finally took place in the fall of 1980.

It is sometimes said that officials should refuse to talk with political terrorists because to do so would confer status and reward their illegal action. It is true that for a high government official to meet with terrorists might well appear to enhance the terrorists' importance to an extent that outweighs the potential gain. But contact at a professional level may be quite different. Urban police negotiators have learned that direct personal dialogue with criminals who are holding hostages frequently results in the hostages being released and the criminals being taken into custody.

During the 1988 hijacking of Kuwait Airways Flight 422, extensive negotiations occurred with the hijackers but over increasingly small issues. The government of Kuwait said flatly at the beginning of the incident that they would not release the hijackers' comrades, who were in jail in Kuwait after having been convicted of terrorist acts, and the government never retreated from that fundamental principle. But local authorities in Cyprus and Algeria negotiated incessantly over things like permission for the plane to land, requests for additional fuel, access to news media, and deliveries of food. For each transaction these authorities successfully obtained the release of more hostages. At the same time, they appealed—as fellow Muslims—to Islamic ideals of mercy and the Prophet Muhammed's admonitions against the taking of hostages. Eventually all the hostages were released. The hijackers were also allowed to leave Algeria, but their prolonged and embarrassing failure to achieve any of their announced goals no doubt contributed to a subsequent reduction in terrorist hijackings.

Negotiate with someone like Hitler? It depends on the alternative. Some interests you have may be worth fighting and even dying for. Many of us feel that ridding the world of fascism, standing up to territorial aggression, and putting a stop to genocide fall into that category. If such interests are at stake and cannot be met by less costly means, you should be prepared to fight if that will help, and—some will say—sometimes even if it won't.

On the other hand, war is a nasty business, too often romanticized. If you *can* achieve a substantial measure of your interests through nonviolent means, you should give that option serious consideration. Few wars are as one-sided as the United Nations liberation of Kuwait. Even there, a negotiated withdrawal of Iraqi forces from Kuwait might have avoided the oil fires in Kuwait, the environmental damage to the Persian Gulf, and the enormous human suffering caused by the war.

Most important, war offers no guarantee of results better than could be achieved by other means. As premier of the Soviet Union, Joseph Stalin was in many ways as objectionable to the world as Hitler had been. He committed a variety of territorial aggressions, engaged in genocide, and promoted a state-centered ideology that in practice looked a lot like National Socialism. But in an age of hydrogen bombs, conquering the Soviet Union as the Allies had conquered Germany in World War II was no longer a viable option. Nor did the principles at stake seem to justify mutual annihilation. Instead, the West waited, patient and steadfast in its moral opposition to Soviet communism, until it collapsed of its own accord.

Even with someone like Hitler or Stalin, we should consider

negotiating if negotiation holds the promise of achieving an outcome that, all things considered, meets our interests better than
our BATNA.* When a war does occur, in many cases it is actually
a move within a negotiation. The violence is intended to change
the other side's BATNA, or their perception of it, so that they will
more readily agree to our terms for peace. In such cases thinking
in negotiation terms is vital so that we do not neglect to craft and
communicate our offer in ways that we can reasonably expect
will be persuasive to the other side.

Negotiate when people are acting out of religious conviction?
Yes. Although people's religious convictions are unlikely to be
changed through negotiation, the actions they take, even those
based on their convictions, *may* be subject to influence. Such was
the case with the Kuwait Airways hijacking. A key point, worth
repeating, is that negotiating does not require compromising
your principles. More often success is achieved by finding a solution that is arguably consistent with each side's principles.

Many situations only appear to be "religious" conflicts. The
conflict in Northern Ireland between Protestants and Catholics,
like the conflict in Lebanon between Christians and Muslims, is
not over religion. In each case, religion serves as a handy boundary line for dividing one group from another. That cleavage is
reinforced as it is used to divide where people live, where they
work, who their friends are, and for whom they vote. Negotiation between such groups is highly desirable, as it improves the
chance that they will be able to reach pragmatic accommoda-
tions that are to their mutual interest.

When does it make sense *not* to negotiate? Whether it makes
sense to negotiate and how much effort to put into it depends on
how satisfactory you find your BATNA and how likely you think
it is that negotiation will produce better results. If your BATNA is

---

* For an in-depth consideration of whether and when to negotiate with unsavory counterparts that draws on a variety of contemporary and historical examples, see Robert Mnookin, *Bargaining with the Devil: When to Negotiate,
When to Fight* (Simon & Schuster, 2010).

fine and negotiation looks unpromising, there is no reason to invest much time in negotiation. On the other hand, if your BATNA is awful, you should be willing to invest a little more time—even where negotiation looks unpromising—to test whether something more satisfactory might be worked out.

To do this analysis, you need to have thought carefully about your BATNA and the other side's. You should not make the mistake of the bank that was negotiating with a bankrupt energy company. Legally, the bank was entitled to take over ownership of the entire company, but the judge in the case said that he wanted the parties to settle. The bank offered to take 51 percent of the stock and reduce the interest on the loan, but the company (owned by management) stonewalled. Frustrated, the bank spent months trying to get the company to show an interest in negotiating. Understandably, the company refused—the company saw their BATNA as merely waiting for oil prices to rise. At that point they could pay off their loan and they would still own 100 percent of their company. The bank had failed to think clearly either about their own BATNA or the company's. The bank should have been negotiating with the *judge*, explaining how this situation was unfair and appealable. (Indeed, once the bank successfully enlisted the judge's help—appealing to his interest in not having to hear the case—the company settled within twenty-four hours.) But the bank thought negotiating with the company was its only choice.

Governments often make the mistake of assuming that they have a better BATNA than they do—for example, when they imply that if "political" and "economic" means fail in a given situation, then there is always "the military option." There is *not* always a viable military option. (Consider most hostage situations, in which there is no military option that can realistically promise the hostages' safe retrieval. Successful rescue raids like that of the Israeli military on the Ugandan airport at Entebbe— an airport designed and built by Israeli engineers—are exceptional and become more difficult with each success, as terrorists adapt to new tactics.) Whether or not we have a self-help option depends on the situation: Can the objective be achieved solely through our own efforts, or will someone on the other side have to make a decision? If the latter, then whose decision will we have to influence, what decision do we want, and how, if at all, could military force help influence that decision?'

Don't assume that you have a BATNA better than negotiating or that you don't. Think it through. Then decide whether negotiating makes sense.

Question 6: "How should I adjust my negotiating approach to account for differences of personality, gender, culture, and so on?"

In some ways people everywhere are similar to one another. We want to be loved, we care about the respect of other people and of ourselves, and we do not like to feel taken advantage of. In other ways, people—even those of similar background—are quite different. Some of us are outgoing, others shy; some verbal and logic-chopping, others more physical and emotive; some people are blunt, others more indirect and tactful; some relish conflict, others will do almost anything to avoid it. As negotiators, different people will have different interests and styles of communication. Different things may be persuasive to them, and they may have different ways of making decisions. How should we accommodate such similarities and differences in negotiating with different people? Here are some suggested guidelines:

Get in step. In any negotiation it is highly desirable to be sensitive to the values, perceptions, concerns, norms of behavior, and mood of those with whom you are dealing. Adapt your behavior accordingly. If you are negotiating with someone, it is that person whom you are trying to affect. The more successfully you can get in step with that person's way of thinking, the more likely you are to be able to work out an agreement. Some common differences that can make a difference in negotiation include the following:

- Pacing: fast or slow?
- Formality: high or low?

- Physical proximity while talking: close or distant?
- Oral or written agreements: which are more binding and inclusive?
- Bluntness of communication: direct or indirect?
- Time frame: short-term or longer?
- Scope of relationship: business-only or all-encompassing?
- The expected place of doing business: private or public?
- Who negotiates: equals in status or the most competent people for the task?
- Rigidity of commitments: written in stone or meant to be flexible?

Adapt our general advice to the specific situation. This is a book of general advice. It will not apply in the same way in every circumstance with every person. But the basic propositions are generally applicable. Absent a compelling reason to do otherwise, we advise crafting your specific approach to every negotiation around them. The best way to *implement* these general principles will depend on the specific context. Consider where you are, with whom you are dealing, customs of the industry, past experience with this negotiator, and so on, in crafting an approach to fit the situation.

Pay attention to differences of belief and custom, but avoid stereotyping individuals. Different groups and places have different customs and beliefs. Know and respect them, but beware of making assumptions about individuals.

The attitudes, interests, and other characteristics of an individual are often quite different from those of a group to which they may belong. For example, the "average" Japanese tends to favor more indirect methods of communication and negotiation, but individual Japanese span the full gamut of negotiating styles. One prominent, long-time minister in the Japanese government was famous for his brash "American-style" negotiating—which is not at all typical of many Americans. Some research suggests that women are more likely than men to gather information in a more open and less structured way, to be more sensitive to relationships, and to operate on a morality that is based proportionately more on caring and obligation to others and less on rules and individual rights. These same data, however, suggest that there are a great many individuals of each sex who tend the other way.*

Making assumptions about someone based on their group characteristics is insulting, as well as factually risky. It denies that person his or her individuality. We do not assume that *our* beliefs and habits are dictated by the groups in which we happen to fit; to imply as much of others is demeaning. Each of us is affected by myriad aspects of our environment and upbringing, our culture and group identity, but in no individually predictable way.

Question your assumptions; listen actively. Whatever assumption you make about others—whether you assume they are just like you or totally different—question it. Be open to learning that they are quite unlike what you expected. The wide variations among cultures provide clues as to the kind of differences for which you should be looking, but remember that all of us have special interests and qualities that do not fit any standard mold.

QUESTIONS ABOUT TACTICS

Question 7: "How do I decide things like 'Where should we meet?' 'How should we communicate?' 'Who should make the first offer?' and 'How high should I start?'"

Before a doctor can answer such questions as what pill to take and what food to avoid, he or she will want to learn about the patient's symptoms and diagnose possible causes. Only then can the doctor develop a general strategy for better health. The same is true for specialists in negotiation. We have no all-purpose patent medicines. Good tactical advice requires knowledge of specific circumstances.

---

* See, as a starting point, Carol Gilligan, *In a Different Voice* (Harvard University Press, 1982).

This can be illustrated by considering four specific examples:

Where should we meet? What are we worried about? If both parties tend to be extremely busy and subject to constant interruptions, seclusion may be the most important consideration. If the other person tends to feel insecure or in need of staff support, perhaps they would be more comfortable meeting in their office. You may also want to meet in the other party's office if you would like to feel free to walk away. Are there charts, files, or technical experts that you might want to be able to consult during the negotiation? If you want to be free to use flip charts, a whiteboard, or an overhead projector, you may want to meet in a conference room that has such facilities.

How should we communicate? Today many negotiations are conducted by phone, email, or text, and the interaction can be quite different than meeting face-to-face. The short length and abbreviations used in texting greatly increase the likelihood of unintended misunderstandings. The lack of audio and visual cues in texts and email make it much harder to hear or interpret the emotional undertones of communication, which can feed our tendency to hear the worst. Furthermore, not having another person in front of us reduces or eliminates the impact of "mirror neurons" in our brain, which normally increase our empathy and sense of human connection with our counterpart.

One study suggests the potential impact of these differences: In a negotiation where only sellers knew what an item was worth, the results varied dramatically based on the mode of communication. In face-to-face interactions, only a small minority of sellers lied and took advantage. But in written interactions a third did and in phone negotiations more than half did. Meanwhile, buyers were appropriately wary in written interactions, but generally trusting in face-to-face and phone negotiations, leading many telephone buyers to be seriously disadvantaged. Almost 60 percent of face-to-face negotiations resulted in mutually beneficial agreements, while only 22 percent did in written interactions and 38 percent in telephone negotiations. Meanwhile, more than half of the written interactions resulted in impasse, while only 19 percent of the face-to-face talks and 14 percent of the telephone negotiations did.*

What are the implications of such differences for strategy? First, difficult conversations involving emotions or relationship issues are best pursued face-to-face, if at all possible, and definitely not by email or text. If a phone call is the only option, consider using a Webcam and an Internet service to make it a video call.

When you are on the phone, and especially when you are using email or texts, make an effort to create some personal connection before diving into substance. Studies show that a little effort up front to schmooze—to learn and share something personal, to evoke an existing relationship or shared identity, or to find a shared connection—helps promote cooperation and increases the chances of agreement. With email or a text, reread your message one or more times before sending. Put in a little extra effort to make the context and your reasoning transparent. Look for ambiguities and ask yourself how the other party could hear something different from what you intend. Then, if a reply suggests that your message *has* possibly generated a bad or unexpected reaction, consider changing your mode of communication before continuing. Walk down the hall, or pick up the phone.

Even if the bulk of your communication needs to be on email, try to have an initial meeting in person or on the phone, and schedule periodic check-ins in the same mode, to create and maintain a level of human connection. It also helps to make some procedural agreements that anticipate possible difficulties. For example, you may want to make a mutual promise to raise even tentative concerns early, in person or by phone, and to raise them as fears, fantasies, or hypotheses, rather than as accusations.

---

* K. L. Valley, J. Moag, and M. H. Bazerman, "'A Matter of Trust': Effects of Communication on the Efficiency and Distribution of Outcomes," 34 *Journal of Economic Behavior and Organization* 211 (1998). For a review of research on modes of communication in negotiation, see J. Nadler and D. Shestowsky, "Negotiation, Information Technology, and the Problem of the Faceless Other," in Leigh L. Thompson, editor, *Negotiation Theory and Research* (Psychology Press, 2006).

Of course, there are occasions where using the phone, email, or texting may be advantageous. Many people find it easier to be less accommodating on the phone, for example, and to ask tougher questions. Research suggests that people pay closer attention to content in the absence of other interpersonal information, and that strong arguments may have more effect by email than face-to-face. Email also allows time for reflection and research before answering, which can help you avoid making unwise decisions under pressure. (Texting, in contrast, tends to move faster and can give "fast talkers" an undeserved edge.)

As always, the choice of how to communicate is something that should emerge from careful preparation, taking into account these kinds of considerations.

Who should make the first offer? It would be a mistake to assume that making an offer is always the best way to put a figure on the table. Usually you will want to explore interests, options, and criteria for a while before making an offer. Making an offer too soon can make the other side feel railroaded. Once both sides have a sense of the problem, an offer that makes an effort to reconcile the interests and standards that have been advanced is more likely to be received as a constructive step forward. (Without that groundwork, even a generous offer may be seen suspiciously as a result of what social psychologists call "reactive devaluation": If you are offering it, it must not be good for me.*)

Whether or not you make an offer, you may want to try to "anchor" the discussion early around an approach or standard favorable to you. On the other hand, if you are ill prepared and have no idea what would be reasonable, you will probably be reluctant to put an idea or an offer on the table, perhaps hoping that the other side will go first and offer something generous. But you should be careful. It is extremely risky to measure the value of an item by the other side's first proposal or figure. If you know

---

* See Jared R. Curhan, Margaret A. Neale, and Lee Ross, "Dynamic Valuation: Preference Changes in the Context of Face-to-Face Negotiations," 40 *Journal of Experimental Social Psychology* 142 (2004).

that little about an item's value, you should probably engage in more research before starting the negotiation.

The better prepared both parties are in a negotiation over price, the less difference it makes who makes the first offer. Rather than learning rules about who should make the first offer, it would be better to learn the rule of being well prepared with external measures of value.

How high should I start? Many people tend to measure success by how far the other party has moved. Even if the first figure is a wholly arbitrary assertion of "sticker price" or "retail value," buyers will often feel happy about getting something for less. They have not checked the market. They do not know what their best alternative would cost, so they derive satisfaction from paying less than the first "asking price."

Under these circumstances, if you are selling, you would ordinarily start with the highest figure that you could justify without embarrassment. Another way to think of it is to start with the highest figure that you would try to persuade a neutral third party was fair. In putting forth such a figure you would first explain the reasoning and then give the number. (If they hear a number they don't like, they may not listen to the reasoning.)

Such an opening figure need not be advanced as a firm position. Indeed, the firmer you suggest early figures to be, the greater you damage your credibility as you move off them. It is safer and at least as effective to say something like "Well, one factor to consider would be what others are paying for comparable work. In New York, for example, they pay $58 an hour. How does that sound?" Here you have put out a standard and a figure without committing to it at all.

Strategy depends on preparation. There are two generalizations about strategy worth passing along. First, in almost all cases, strategy is a function of preparation. If you are well prepared, a strategy will suggest itself. If you are well versed in the standards relevant to your negotiation, it will be obvious which ones to discuss and which ones the other side might raise. If you have thoroughly considered your interests, it will be clear which ones to mention early on and which ones to bring up later or not at all. And if you have formulated your BATNA in advance, you'll know when it's time to walk.

Second, a clever strategy cannot make up for lack of preparation. If you formulate a step-by-step strategy that is sure to knock their socks off, you will run into trouble when they come into the negotiation wearing sandals. Your strategy might depend on discussing relationship issues at the beginning, but they might want to talk about BATNAs. Because you can never be sure what their strategy will be, it is far better to know the terrain than to plan on taking one particular path through the woods.

Question 8: "Concretely, how do I move from inventing options to making commitments?"

We have offered a great deal of advice on how to develop wise, mutually satisfying options in negotiation and how to avoid or overcome a variety of people problems. The question remains, how do you reach closure on issues? We don't believe that there is any one best process, but here are some general principles worth considering:

Think about closure from the beginning. Before you even begin to negotiate, it makes sense to envision what a successful agreement might look like. This will help you figure out what issues will need to be dealt with in the negotiation and what it might take to resolve them. Imagine what it might be like to implement an agreement. What issues would need to be resolved? Then work backward. Ask yourself how the other side might successfully explain and justify an agreement to their constituents. ("We will be in the top 10 percent of all electrical workers in Ontario." "We are paying less than the value given by two out of three appraisers.") Think about what it will take for you to do the same. Then ask yourself what kind of an agreement would allow you both to say such things. Finally, think about what it might take to persuade the other side—and you—to accept a proposed agreement, rather than continuing to negotiate.

Keep these questions in mind as your negotiation progresses, reshaping and filling in your vision as more information becomes available. Focusing on your goal in this way will help to keep your negotiation on a productive track.

Consider crafting a framework agreement. In negotiations that will produce a written agreement, it is usually a good idea to sketch the outlines of what an agreement might look like as part of your preparation. Such a "framework agreement" is a document in the form of an agreement, but with blank spaces for each term to be resolved by negotiation. The standard purchase-and-sale form that is available from any real-estate broker is an example of a detailed framework agreement. In other cases nothing more than a list of headings may be appropriate. Working out a framework agreement, however detailed, will help ensure that important issues are not overlooked during the negotiation. Such an agreement can serve as a starting point and an agenda for the negotiation, helping you to use your time efficiently.

Whether or not you start your negotiation with a framework agreement, it makes sense to draft possible terms of an agreement as you go. Working on a draft helps to keep discussions focused, tends to surface important issues that might otherwise be overlooked, and gives a sense of progress. Drafting as you go also provides a record of discussions, reducing the chance of later misunderstanding. If you are working with a framework agreement, drafting may involve no more than filling in the blanks as you discuss each term; or, if you have yet to reach consensus, it may involve drafting alternative provisions.

Move toward commitment gradually. As the negotiation proceeds and you discuss options and standards for each issue, you should be seeking a consensus proposal that reflects all the points made and meets each side's interests on that issue as well as possible. If you are as yet unable to reach consensus on a single option, try at least to narrow the range of options under consideration and then go on to another issue. Perhaps a better option or a trade-off possibility will occur later. ("All right. So perhaps something like $68,000 or $70,000 might make sense on salary. What about starting date?")

To encourage brainstorming, it is a good idea to agree explicitly that all commitments are tentative. This will allow you to have some sense of progress during your discussions, while avoiding the inhibiting effect of worrying that every option discussed may be heard as a commitment. Tentative commitments are fine and should not be changed without reason. But make clear that you are not firmly committing yourself to anything until you see the final package. At the top of a framework agreement, for example, you might write: "Tentative Draft—No Commitments."

The process of moving toward agreement is seldom linear. Be prepared to move through the list of issues several times, going back and forth between looking at particular issues and the total package. Difficult issues may be revisited frequently or set aside until the end, depending on whether incremental progress seems possible. Along the way, avoid demands or locking in. Instead, offer options and ask for criticism. ("What would you think of an agreement along the lines of this draft? I am not sure I could sell it to my people, but it might be in the ballpark. Could something like this work for you? If not, what would be wrong with it?")

Be persistent in pursuing your interests but not rigid in pursuing any particular solution. One way to be firm without being positional is to separate your interests from ways to meet them. When a proposal is challenged, don't defend the proposal; rather explain again your underlying interests. Ask if the other side can think of a better way to meet those interests, as well as their own. If there appears to be an irresolvable conflict, ask if there is any reason why one side's interests should have priority over the other's.

Unless the other side makes a persuasive case for why your thinking is incomplete and should be changed, stick to your analysis. When and if you are persuaded, modify your thinking accordingly, presenting the logic first. ("Well, that's a good point. One way to measure that factor would be to . . . .") If you have prepared well, you should have anticipated most arguments the other side might raise and thought through how you think they should affect the result.

Throughout, the goal is to avoid useless quarreling. Where disagreements persist, seek second-order agreement—agreement on where you disagree. Make sure that each side's interests and reasoning are clear. Seek differing assumptions and ways to test them. As always seek to reconcile conflicting interests with external standards or creative options. Seek to reconcile conflicting standards with criteria for evaluating which is more appropriate or with creative trade-offs. Be persistent.

Make an offer. At some point clarifying interests, inventing options, and analyzing standards produce diminishing returns. Once an issue or group of issues is well explored, you should be prepared to make an offer. An early offer might be limited to the pairing of a couple of key issues. ("I would agree to a June 30 closing if the down payment were not more than $50,000.") Later, such partial offers can be combined into a more comprehensive proposal.

Usually an offer should not come as a surprise. It should be a natural outgrowth of the discussion so far. It need not be a "take-it-or-leave-it" proposal, but neither should it be an opening position. It should be an offer that you think would make sense for both sides, given what has gone before. Many negotiations settle when a complete offer is made.

You should give some thought to how and where you convey an offer. If discussions have been carried on publicly or in large groups, you may want to seek a more private occasion for exploring final commitments. Most agreements are made in one-on-one meetings between the top negotiators for each side, although formal closure may come later in a more public forum.

If agreement makes sense but some issues remain stubbornly in dispute, look for fair procedures to facilitate closure. Splitting the difference between arbitrary figures produces an arbitrary result. But splitting the difference between figures that are each backed by legitimate and persuasive independent standards is one way to find a fair result. Another approach, where differences persist, is for one or both parties to invite a third party to talk with each side and, perhaps after repeated consultations, produce a final "last chance" recommendation.

Be generous at the end. When you sense you are finally close to an agreement, consider giving the other side something you know to be of value to them and still consistent with the basic logic of your proposal. Make clear that this is a final gesture; you do not want to raise expectations of further concessions. Such an improved offer can sometimes break through any last-minute doubts and clinch the deal.

You want the other side to leave the negotiation feeling satisfied and fairly treated. That feeling can pay off handsomely in the implementation of an agreement as well as in future negotiations.

Question 9: "How do I try out these ideas without taking too much risk?"

Perhaps you are persuaded that this approach makes sense but are worried that you will not be able to execute it well enough to better the results of your current approach. What can you do to try out these ideas without taking too much risk?

Start small. Experiment in negotiations where the stakes are small, where you have a good BATNA, where favorable objective standards are available and seem relevant, and where the other side is likely to be amenable to this approach. Start with ideas that build on your current skills, then try out new ideas one at a time. As you gain experience and confidence, slowly raise the stakes by trying new techniques in more significant and challenging contexts. You don't have to try everything at once.

Make an investment. Some people play tennis all their lives but never get better. Those people are not willing to take a fresh look at what they do or to consider changing it. Good players recognize that getting better often means making an investment in new approaches. For a while they may get worse as they wrestle with new and unfamiliar techniques, but eventually they surpass their old plateau. The new techniques offer more long-term potential. You need to do the same with negotiation.

Review your performance. Schedule time to think about how you did after each significant negotiation. What worked? What did not? What might you have done differently? Consider keeping a negotiation journal or diary, which you can reread periodically.

Prepare! Negotiation power, as discussed below, is not something of which you have a certain quantity that can be applied anywhere for any purpose. It requires hard work in advance to bring your resources to bear on being persuasive in a particular situation. In other words, it requires preparation. There is no risk in being well prepared. It simply takes time. The better prepared you are, the more likely you are to use these ideas and to find them of value.

Plan how to build and maintain a good working relationship with the other side. Write out a list of your interests and the other side's. Then invent a list of options that might satisfy as many of these interests as possible. Look for a variety of external benchmarks or criteria that might persuade a reasonable third party of what should be done. Ask yourself what arguments you would like to be able to make, and then see if you can't find the facts and information you would need to make them. Also consider what benchmarks your counterpart might find persuasive in justifying an agreement to his or her constituents. If negotiators for the other side would find it difficult to justify terms to their constituents, agreement on those terms is unlikely. And consider what commitments you would like each side to make. Sketch out a possible framework agreement.

In some cases you may want to ask a friend to help you role-play an upcoming negotiation, either by playing the other side or by playing you (after coaching) while you play the other side. (Assuming the role of the other side and listening from the receiving end to your own arguments is a powerful technique for testing your case.) You may also want to seek coaching from friends, more experienced negotiators, or professional negotiation consultants.

In many ways, negotiation is like athletics: Some people have more natural talent, and like the best athletes, they may gain the most from preparation, practice, and coaching. Yet those with less natural talent have more need for preparation, practice, and feedback, and much to gain by it. Whichever you are, there is much to learn, and hard work will pay off. It is up to you.

QUESTIONS ABOUT POWER

Question 10: "Can the way I negotiate really make a difference if the other side is more powerful?" And "How do I enhance *my* negotiating power?"

How you negotiate (and how you prepare to negotiate) can make an *enormous* difference, whatever the relative strengths of each party.

Some things you can't get

Of course, no matter how skilled you are, there are limits to what you can get through negotiation. The best negotiator in the world will not be able to buy the White House. You should not expect success in negotiation unless you are able to make the other side an offer they find more attractive than their BATNA — their Best Alternative To a Negotiated Agreement. If that seems impossible, then negotiation doesn't make sense. Concentrate instead on improving your BATNA and perhaps changing theirs.

How you negotiate makes a big difference

In a situation where there *is* a chance for agreement, the way you negotiate can make the difference between coming to terms and not, or between an outcome that you find favorable and one that is merely acceptable. How you negotiate may determine whether the pie is expanded or merely divided, and whether you have a good relationship with the other side or a strained one. When the other side seems to hold all the cards, how you negotiate is absolutely critical. Suppose, for example, that you are negotiating for an exception to a rule or a job offer. Realistically, you may have little recourse if the other side denies your request and little to offer if they grant it. In this situation, your negotiation skill is everything. However small the opportunity for success, the way in which you negotiate will determine whether you are able to take advantage of it.

"Resources" are not the same as "negotiation power"

Negotiation power is the ability to persuade someone to do something. The United States is rich and has lots of nuclear bombs, but neither has been of much help in deterring terrorist actions or freeing hostages when they have been held in places like Beirut. Whether your resources give you negotiating power will depend on the context—on whom you are trying to persuade and what you want them to do.

Don't ask "Who's more powerful?"

Trying to estimate whether you or your counterparts are more "powerful" is risky. If you conclude that you are more powerful, you may relax and not prepare as well as you should. On the other hand, if you conclude that you are weaker than the other side, there is a risk that you will be discouraged and again not devote sufficient attention to how you might persuade them. Whatever you conclude will not help you figure out how best to proceed.

In fact, a great deal can be done to enhance your negotiation power even when the resource balance is one-sided. Of course, there will be negotiations where, at least in the short term, the best cards are held by the other side. But in this increasingly interdependent world, there are almost always resources and potential allies that a skilled and persistent negotiator can exploit, at least to move the fulcrum, if not ultimately to tip the balance of power the other way. You won't find out what's possible unless you try.

Sometimes people seem to prefer feeling powerless and believing that there is nothing they can do to affect a situation. That belief helps them avoid feeling responsible or guilty about inaction. It also avoids the costs of trying to change the situation—making an effort and risking failure, which might cause the person embarrassment. But while this feeling is understandable, it does not affect the reality of what the person might accomplish by effective negotiation. It is a self-defeating and self-fulfilling attitude.

The best rule of thumb is to be optimistic—to let your reach exceed your grasp. Without wasting a lot of resources on hopeless causes, recognize that many things are worth trying for even if you may not succeed. The more you try for, the more you are likely to get. Studies of negotiation consistently show a strong correlation between aspiration and result. Within reason, it pays to think positively.

There are many sources of negotiation power

How do you enhance your negotiating power? This whole book is an attempt to answer that question. Negotiation power has many sources. One is having a good BATNA. Provided they believe you, it is persuasive to tell the other side that you have a better alternative. But each of the four elements of the method outlined in Part II of this book—people (the relationship), interests, options, and objective criteria—is also a source of negotiation power. If the other side is strong in one area, you can try to develop strength in another. To these five we would now add a sixth, the power of commitment, and seventh, the power of effective communication, including process management.

There is power in developing a good working relationship between the people negotiating. If you understand the other side and they understand you; if emotions are acknowledged and people are treated with respect even when they disagree; if there is clear, two-way communication with good listening; if there is mutual trust and confidence in one another's reliability; and if people problems are dealt with directly on their merits, not by demanding or offering concessions on substance, negotiations are likely to be smoother and more successful for both parties. In this sense, negotiation power is not a zero-sum phenomenon. More negotiation power for the other side does not necessarily mean less for you. The better your working relationship, the better able each of you is to influence the other.

Contrary to some conventional wisdom, you will often benefit from the other side's increasing their ability to influence you. Two people with well-deserved reputations for being trustworthy are each better able to influence the other than are two people with reputations for dishonesty. That you can trust the other side increases their ability to influence you. But you also benefit. You can safely enter into agreements that will benefit both sides.

When the British ambassador to the United Nations, Lord Caradon, was seeking agreement on a Security Council resolution to set a framework for peace in the Middle East after the 1967 war, it appeared he had consensus except for the Soviet vote. The Soviet representative, Vasily Kuznetsov, approached Caradon to request a delay in the vote for two days. Caradon resisted, fearing that the Soviets would use the delay to win more votes for their alternative resolution. Kuznetsov persisted, "You may have misunderstood me. I am *personally* asking you for two days." As soon as Caradon heard the word "personal," he knew he had to grant Kuznetsov his wish. Why? "I knew Kuznetsov very well. I had worked with him on other difficult issues. I greatly respected him. I knew he could not work against me. . . . I knew I could trust him as he could trust me." So Caradon went to the Security Council and requested a delay in the vote. Two days later the Security Council met to vote. "I raised my hand to vote," recalled Caradon. "And then there was a cheer from the galleries. I looked to my right and saw Kuznetsov's finger raised voting for our resolution and withdrawing his own, thus making the vote for the British Resolution 242 unanimous. He had made good use of the two days. He had come to the conclusion that a unanimous vote and full agreement were essential. He had gone back to his Government and, I have no doubt, to Arab Governments, too, and he had persuaded them."* U.N. Resolution 242 remains central to Middle East peace negotiations to this day.

---

* Quoted in Karen A. Feste, *Plans for Peace: Negotiation and the Arab–Israeli Conflict* (Greenwood Press, 1991).

Kuznetsov's example shows the power of a trustworthy reputation, even independent of the organization you may represent. Your reputation for honesty and fair-dealing may be your single most important asset as a negotiator.

There is power in effective communication. Good communication is an especially significant source of negotiating power. Crafting your message with punch, listening to the other side, and showing that you have heard can all increase your persuasiveness. Skillfully managing the negotiation process—making game-changing moves as needed—can dramatically affect the quality of the outcome you achieve.

President John F. Kennedy was justly famous for his skill at the first of these, crafting a forceful message: "Let us never negotiate out of fear. But let us never fear to negotiate."[*]

A message does not have to be unequivocal to be clear and effective. In many cases, helping the other side understand your thinking—even when you are of two minds about something— can reduce their fears, clear up misperceptions, and promote joint problem-solving. Consider the supplier who makes what she thinks is a competitive bid for a business supply contract. The purchaser likes the bid and the bidder but is worried that the bidder's firm, which is new to the market, may not be able to manage the volume needed to meet his peak requirements. If the purchaser says simply, "No, thank you" and then pays more to hire another firm, the bidder may assume that the purchaser disliked her bid. And the bidder would have no opportunity to persuade the purchaser that she could handle the needed volume. It would be better for both if, instead, the purchaser shared both his interest in the bid and his concerns.

Good listening can increase your negotiation power by increasing the information you have about the other side's interests or about possible options. Once you understand the other side's

---

[*] Inaugural Address, January 20, 1961.

feelings and concerns, you can begin to address them, to explore areas of agreement and disagreement, and to develop useful ways to proceed in the future. Consider, for example, the elderly man whose doctors wanted to move him from his current hospital to one with specialized facilities. The doctors repeatedly explained how the specialized hospital would be better for him, but the man refused to budge. Knowing that the man was acting against his own best interests, the doctors dismissed his reasoning as irrational. One intern, however, took the man seriously and listened carefully to why he did not want to move. The patient told of how he had suffered repeated abandonments in his life and his fears that moving might result in another. The intern set about addressing this concern directly, and the man happily agreed to be moved.

Showing that you have heard the other side also increases your ability to persuade them. When the other side feels heard *by* you, they are more apt to listen *to* you. It is comparatively easy to listen when the other side is saying something that you agree with. It is harder to listen to things with which you disagree, but that is the very time it is most effective. Listen before you launch into a rebuttal. Inquire. Make sure you understand their view, and make sure they know you understand. Once the other side knows that you understand what they have said, they cannot dismiss your disagreement as simple lack of understanding.

Your awareness of negotiation process and your ability to make game-changing moves increases your negotiation power because the process of the negotiation affects the kind of outcomes you can achieve. Positional bargaining frequently results in odd, arbitrary results that are difficult to explain to constituents and of little value as precedents in future negotiations. It also tends to bruise relationships.

As discussed in Chapter 8, recognizing a tactic or move allows you to name it and begin an explicit negotiation over process. Another way to "change the game" is to change the frame. In other words, move the focus in the negotiation from positions to interests, options, or standards. If the other side says, for example, "$10,000 is the most we will pay," when you think $50,000 would be fair, you could respond in several ways:

- **Reframe to interests:** "I hear that is your position. Given how far that seems below the market price, help me understand your interests. Are you experiencing a serious cash flow crisis?"
- **Reframe to options:** "$10,000 is one option, just as $100,000 or $200,000 would be attractive options from our point of view. I think we'll get a lot further brainstorming options likely to be acceptable and attractive to both of us. What if we were to . . . ?"
- **Reframe to standards:** "You must have good reasons for thinking $10,000 is a fair offer. How did you arrive at that number? Why that number, instead of, say, $0 or $100,000? My understanding is that the market price is $50,000. Why should we agree on less?"
- **Reframe to BATNA:** "Of course, that's your decision to make, and perhaps someone else will accept that. I think we need to think hard now about whether an agreement is possible here that would make sense for both of us."

One of the greatest powers you have is to reframe, using statements and questions to change the focus of negotiation to interests, options, and standards — and thus to change the game from positional bargaining to principled negotiation.*

Let's return to the neighbors from Chapter 3 who are concerned about an unwanted and unsafe construction site. Consider the difference between beginning their negotiation with the construction company by saying, "We demand that a fence be built around the site immediately!" or instead beginning, "I have a simple question for you: Does your company adhere to

---

* For more on reframing and other strategies for negotiating in difficult situations, see William Ury, *Getting Past No: Negotiating in Difficult Situations* (Bantam, 1991; revised edition 1993).

industry standards of safety?" That is certainly a question to which the company cannot afford to answer "no." And once they say "yes," the neighbors only need standards collected from competitor companies to make their point persuasively, and on the merits. "Well, Turner Construction said they would put a two-meter-high fence around anything bigger than a pothole, and always *before* beginning any construction activity."

There is power in understanding interests. The more clearly you understand the other side's concerns, the better able you will be to satisfy them at minimum cost to yourself. Look for intangible or hidden interests that may be important. With concrete interests like money, ask what lies behind them. ("For what will the money be used?") Sometimes even the most firmly stated and unacceptable position reflects an underlying interest that is compatible with your own.

Consider the businessman who was trying to buy a radio station. The majority owner was willing to sell his two-thirds of the station for a reasonable figure, but the one-third owner (and current manager of the station) was demanding what seemed an exorbitant price for her third. The businessman had raised his offer several times to no avail, and he was beginning to consider abandoning the deal. Finally, the businessman inquired more deeply into the second owner's interests. He learned that the second owner had less interest in money than she did in continuing to manage a radio station of which she was a part owner. The businessman offered to buy only that portion of the owner's share he needed for tax reasons and to keep her on as manager. The second owner accepted this offer at a price that saved the businessman almost a million dollars. Understanding the seller's underlying interests had greatly enhanced the buyer's negotiating power.

There is power in inventing an elegant option. Successful brainstorming increases your ability to influence others. Once you understand the interests of each side, it is often possible—as in the radio-station example above—to invent a clever way of having those interests dovetail. Sometimes this can be done by devising an ingenious process option.

Consider the sealed-bid stamp auction. The auctioneer would like bidders to offer the most they might conceivably be willing to pay for the stamps in question. Each potential buyer, however, does not want to pay more than necessary. In a regular sealed-bid auction each bidder tries to offer slightly more than their best guess of what others will bid, which is often less than the bidder would be willing to pay. But in a stamp auction the rules state that the highest bidder gets the stamps at the price of the *second*-highest bid. Buyers can safely bid *exactly* as much as they would be willing to pay to get the stamps, because the auctioneer guarantees that *they will not have to pay it!* No bidder is left wishing that he or she had bid more, and the high bidder is happy to pay less than was offered. The auctioneer is happy knowing that the difference between the highest and second-highest bids is usually smaller than the overall increase in the level of bids under this system versus a regular sealed-bid auction.*

There is power in using external standards of legitimacy. You can use standards of legitimacy both as a sword to persuade others, and as a shield to help you resist pressure to give in arbitrarily. ("I would like to give you a discount, but this price is firm. It is what General Motors paid for the same item last week; here is the bill of sale.") Just as, by finding relevant precedent and principles a lawyer enhances his or her ability to persuade a judge, so a negotiator can enhance his or her negotiation power by finding precedents, principles, and other external criteria of fairness and by thinking of ways to present them forcefully and tellingly: "I am asking for no more and no less than you are paying others for comparable work." "We will pay what the house

---

* A process similar to this can be used in all kinds of allocation decisions, even when the issue is as volatile as where to site a hazardous waste facility. See Howard Raiffa, "Creative Compensation: Maybe 'In My Backyard.'" 1 *Negotiation Journal* 197 (1985).

is worth if we can afford it. We are offering what the similar house nearby sold for last month. Unless you can give us a good reason why your house is worth more, our offer remains firm and unchanged." Convincing the other side that you are asking for no more than is fair is one of the most powerful arguments you can make.

There is power in developing a good BATNA. As we argue in Chapter 6, a fundamental way to increase your negotiation power is by improving your walk-away alternative. An attractive BATNA is a strong argument with which to persuade the other side of the need to offer more. ("The firm across the street has offered me 20 percent above what I am now earning. I would rather stay here. But with the cost of living, unless I can get a good raise soon, I will have to consider moving on. What do you think might be possible?")

In addition to improving your overall BATNA (what you will do if the negotiations fail to produce an agreement), you should also prepare your "micro-BATNA"—if no agreement is reached *at this meeting*, what is the best outcome? It helps to draft in advance a good exit line to use if a meeting is inconclusive. ("Thank you for sharing your views and for listening to mine. If I decide to go forward, I will get back to you, perhaps with a fresh proposal.")

Sometimes it is possible, quite legitimately, to worsen the other side's BATNA. For example, a father we know was trying to get his young son to mow the lawn. He offered a significant amount of money, but to no avail. Finally, the son inadvertently revealed his BATNA: "But Dad, I don't need to mow the lawn to get money. You, uh, leave your wallet on the dresser every weekend. . . ." The father quickly changed his son's BATNA by not leaving his wallet out and making clear that he disapproved of taking money without asking; the son started mowing the lawn. The tactic of worsening the other side's BATNA can be used to coerce or exploit, but it can also help ensure a fair outcome. Efforts to improve one's own alternatives and to lower the other side's estimate of theirs are critical ways to enhance our negotiating power.

There is power in making a carefully crafted commitment. One additional source of persuasive power deserves attention: the power of making commitments. You can use a commitment to enhance your negotiating power in three ways: You can commit to what you will do, for example, by making a firm offer. You can, with care, make a negative commitment as to what you will not do. And you can clarify precisely what commitments you would like the other side to make.

Clarify what you will do. One way to enhance your negotiating power is to make a firm, well-timed offer. When you make a firm offer, you provide one option that you *will* accept, making it clear at the same time that you are not foreclosing discussion of other options. If you want to persuade someone to accept a job, don't just talk about it; make an offer. By making an offer you give up your chance to haggle for better terms. But you gain by simplifying the other side's choice and making it easier for them to commit. To reach agreement, all they have to say is "yes."

Making an offer of what you will do if they agree to the terms you are proposing is one way to overcome any fear the other side may have of starting down a slippery slope. Without a clear offer, even a painful situation may seem preferable to accepting "a pig in a poke," especially if the other side fears that a favorable indication will encourage you to ask for more. In 1990, the U.N. Security Council sought to influence Iraq to withdraw from its military occupation of Kuwait by imposing sanctions. The Council's resolutions clearly stated that Iraq must withdraw, but did *not* state that upon withdrawal sanctions would end. If Iraqi President Saddam Hussein believed that sanctions would continue even after Iraq withdrew from Kuwait, then those sanctions, though unpleasant, provided no incentive for Iraq to leave.

The more concrete the offer, the more persuasive. Thus a written offer may be more credible than an oral one. (A real-estate agent we know likes to have a client make an offer by stacking bundles of hundred-dollar bills on the table.) You may also want to make your offer a "fading opportunity" by indicating when and how it will expire. For example, President Ronald Reagan's inauguration in 1981 created a fading opportunity in the negotiations for the release of the American diplomatic hostages held in Iran. The Iranians did not want to have to start negotiating again with a new U.S. administration.

In some cases, you may also want to clarify what you will do if the other side does not accept your proposal. They may not realize the consequences of your BATNA for them. ("If we can't get heat in our apartment this evening, I will have to call the health department's emergency line. Are you aware that they charge landlords a $250 fine when they respond and find a violation of the statute?")

Consider committing to what you will not do. Sometimes you can persuade the other side to accept an offer better than their BATNA by convincing them that you cannot or will not offer more ("Take it or leave it"). You not only make an offer; you tie your hands against changing it. As discussed in Chapter 1, locking into a position has significant costs; locking in early limits communication and runs the risk of damaging the relationship by making the other side feel ignored or coerced. There is less risk in locking in after you have come to understand the other side's interests and have explored options for joint gains, and it will do less damage to your relationship with the other side if there are credible reasons independent of your will to explain and justify your rigidity.

At some point, it may be best to put a final offer on the table and mean it. Doing so tends to influence the other side by worsening their micro-BATNA. At this point if they say "no," they no longer have open the possibility of reaching a better agreement with you.

Clarify what you want them to do. It pays to think through the precise terms of the commitment you want the other side to make. This ensures that your demand makes sense. "Susan, promise *never* to interrupt me again when I am on the telephone" could easily be disastrous if Susan took her promise literally in an emergency. You want to avoid a sloppy commitment that is overbroad, fails to bind the other side, leaves out crucial information, or is not operational.

Especially when you want the other side to *do* something, it makes sense to tell them exactly what it is you want them to do. Otherwise they may do nothing, not wanting to do more than they have to. In the fall of 1990, for example, the ability of the United States to influence Saddam Hussein was undercut by ambiguity about what would satisfy the United States. At different times, the withdrawal of Iraqi troops from Kuwait, the destruction of Iraqi nuclear facilities, the dismantling of Iraq's military capability, and the overthrow of Saddam Hussein all seemed to be possible U.S. goals.

Make the most of your potential power

To make the most of your potential negotiating power, you should use each source of power in harmony with other sources. Negotiators sometimes look for their strongest source of power and try to use it alone. For example, if a negotiator has a strong BATNA, he or she may confront the other side with it, threatening to walk away unless the last offer is accepted. This is likely to detract from the persuasive power of the negotiator's arguments about why the offer is fair. If you are going to communicate your BATNA, it would be better to do so in ways that respect the relationship, leave open the possibility of two-way communication, underscore the legitimacy of your last offer, suggest how that offer meets the other side's interests, and so forth. The total impact of such negotiation power as you have will be greater if each element is used in ways that reinforce the others.

You will also be more effective as a negotiator if you believe in what you are saying and doing. Whatever use you are able to make of the ideas in this book, don't wear them as though you were wearing someone else's clothes. Cut and fit what we say until you find an approach that both makes sense and is comfortable for you. This may require experimentation and a period of adjustment that is not so comfortable, but in the end, you are likely to maximize your negotiation power if you believe what you say and say what you believe.

Analytical
Table of Contents

III. YES, BUT . . .

IV. IN CONCLUSION

V. TEN QUESTIONS PEOPLE ASK ABOUT GETTING TO YES

A Note on the Harvard Negotiation Project

The Harvard Negotiation Project's mission is to improve the theory, teaching, and practice of negotiation and dispute resolution, so that people can deal more constructively with conflicts ranging from the interpersonal to the international. The Project is part of the Program on Negotiation at Harvard Law School, a consortium of scholars and projects from Harvard, Massachusetts Institute of Technology, Simmons, and Tufts. The work of the Harvard Negotiation Project routinely moves back and forth between the worlds of theory and practice to develop ideas that practitioners find useful and scholars sound. The Project's activities include:

Theory building. The Project has helped to develop frameworks such as the method of principled negotiation summarized in this book. Other frameworks include the method of breakthrough negotiation developed for dealing with difficult people and difficult situations, summarized in *Getting Past No*; a framework for understanding what makes difficult conversations more or less productive, presented in *Difficult Conversations*; a method for understanding and managing emotions in negotiation, described in *Beyond Reason*; systematic tools for getting results, whether in business or international diplomacy, summed up in *Beyond Machiavelli* and *Getting It DONE*; and a method for saying no effectively without destroying the deal or the relationship, described in *The Power of a Positive No*. The Project has also developed such ideas as the one-text mediation procedure used by the United States in the Middle East peace negotiations at Camp David in September 1978.

Education and training. The Project develops programs for professionals (lawyers, businesspeople, diplomats, journalists, government officials, union leaders, military officers, and others) as well as for graduate and undergraduate students and has developed a pilot curriculum for high school students. Each year the Project offers three week-long negotiation courses to lawyers and the general public as part of the Harvard Negotiation Institute. Faculty also teach in the Program on Negotiation for Senior Executives. See *www.pon.harvard.edu.*

Publications. In addition to the many books mentioned above, the Project prepares practical materials, such as *International Mediation: A Working Guide*, checklists for negotiators, case studies, negotiation exercises, teacher's guides, and forms designed to be of use to practitioners, teachers, and students. Inquiries about teaching materials available for distribution should be directed to the Program on Negotiation Clearinghouse.

Action research. Faculty and students actively study ongoing conflicts and occasionally participate as third party advisers and facilitators. The Project has contributed to U.S.–Soviet détente, the Central American peace process, the South African constitutional negotiations and the political negotiations that preceded them, and many other situations. Currently, one effort underway is Abraham's Path (Masar Ibrahim al Khalil), an initiative that seeks to build mutual understanding and respect between the West and the Muslim world by inspiring travel in the Middle East along the ancient route of Abraham, the progenitor of many peoples and faiths.